PUBLIC HEALTH/ PERSONAL DISEASE

A Memoir

Denise Simons-Morton, MD, MPH, PhD

To Sam
From Denise

Independently published, Kindle Direct Publishing (v3.3)

ISBN: 978-1-0761-9627-9

Cover photo by the author

AUTHOR'S NOTE: The stories in this memoir are true. Dialogue in quotes conveys the gist of conversations, not the exact words, as I made no recordings, took few notes, and did not keep a journal. For confidentiality, I don't use full names, changed a few names, and occasionally don't use a name at all. I realize that some people may not remember events the same way I do, but I portray things the way I remember them, as truthfully as possible.

"You should be able to explain your research to a twelve-year-old."

Donald G. Simons, Phd

CONTENTS

PROLOGUE

I'm sitting at a large oval table in a conference room along with a dozen professionals from several institutes at the National Institutes of Health. My new job is to chair a committee on how to move results from NIH-funded research into practice. I'm leading a discussion about our mission.

I wake up. I was talking in my sleep.

It's five a.m.

I get up and walk to the bathroom. My left hand is shaking. My shoulder is stiff. My leg aches. I'm unsteady on my feet.

My Parkinson's medication has worn off.

I take my meds, then crawl back into bed. There is no such position. There is no such committee. I have no job to get to.

PART I: DOING OKAY, FOR A GIRL

"The mind is not a vessel to be filled, but a fire to be kindled."

— Plutarch

Animals & Atoms

Mr. Sell, a mostly-bald, white, middle-aged man with a pockmarked red face—and my sixth-grade teacher —stood at the blackboard with chalk in his hand, while we, his students, sat at our desks and watched him. "Animals with backbones are called vertebrates," he said as he wrote the word 'vertebrates' on the board. "All together now, say vertebrates."

We all said, "vertebrates."

"Animals without backbones are called invertebrates," he said as he wrote the word 'invertebrates' on the board. "Now all together say 'invertebrates.'"

We all said, "invertebrates."

It was 1963, the year Martin Luther King, Jr. would give his "I have a dream" speech, President Kennedy would be assassinated, and Betty Friedan would publish "The Feminine Mystique." But I would know nothing about these things until later. Right now, I was intensely interested in what Mr. Sell was writing on the blackboard.

Under the word "invertebrates," Mr. Sell wrote a list: 'sponges, mollusks, segmented worms, arthropods, flatworms, round worms.' There sure were a lot of worms! Mollusks are snails, slugs, squids, and octopuses. Arthropods are spiders, mites, crabs, and insects. Insects have six legs—if they don't have exactly six legs, they are not insects! And they have an exoskeleton. That means they don't have bones; instead they have a hard outside.

Under the word "vertebrates," Mr. Sell wrote another list: 'fish, reptiles, birds, mammals.' All those animals have backbones, a spinal cord inside their backbone, and an inside skeleton. Mammals include dogs and cats and even whales. Mammals also include primates, which are monkeys, apes, chimps, …and humans.

My grandmother, who we called Sittee, had told me that humans aren't animals and that God had put all the animals on Earth for us to use. But there they were—humans—on Mr. Sell's list of animals, in the vertebrate list! (Years later, when I became a vegetarian, I told my Sittee that I don't eat animals, and she said, "Fish aren't animals. Have some fish.")

Mr. Sell handed out mimeographed copies of a tree that had names of the major groups of animals—the animal phyla—on branches of the tree. All the branches came from the same trunk, which showed they were all related, connected somehow in the past. Our assignment was to create a notebook about animals. We were to include the tree, outlines that listed the various types of animals within each phylum, and pictures of animals. It was due in three weeks.

My dad was leaning back in his chair, reading the newspaper as I entered the living room of our small suburban house where I lived with my parents and three sisters. A second-generation Lebanese-American, he had an olive complexion, neatly trimmed black hair, and a small black mustache with skin showing in the middle (the style at the time). "Can I work on my project in here, Daddy?" I asked.

"Sure. Just make sure you clean up your mess when you finish," he said when he saw my arms full of supplies. I sat down on the floor and spread out a few magazines, a pair of scissors, colored pencils, tape, a stapler, tracing and regular paper, and got to work. I was so interested in the topic that I didn't wait until the last minute and cry the night before it was due like I usually did for school projects. I spent hours looking for animal pictures in magazines, tracing some with colored pencils and cutting others out, taping them onto pages in my notebook in the correct section for their animal phylum. So far, I had pictures of an ameba, a sponge, a turtle, an ant, a snake, lots of birds, an elephant, a gazelle, and a monkey. And the circulatory system of a human.

As I worked, I told my dad stuff, often in the form of questions: "Daddy, did you know a sponge is an animal? Did you know coral is too, and barnacles?" or "Wow, an anemone is an animal, but it looks like a plant! Did you know anemones catch fish and eat them?"

After I finished, I held my report high. "I'm done!" It was a long report for a 12-year-old—over 100 pages. I thought it was a masterpiece.

I still do—I have saved it for over 50 years. (I got an A.)

Mr. Sell taught us a lot about science. For physics, I learned that atoms have a nucleus of protons and neutrons, and electrons swirl around the nucleus—the "planetary model" of the atom. Much later I learned about electron shells, that each shell can hold only a certain number of electrons, and that there isn't continuous energy from one shell to another, but the energy is in "quanta," with only certain values of energy permitted. And I learned that light can be both waves and particles at the same time, and so can electrons. My dad, an experimental physicist, told me that protons and neutrons are made up of quarks—up quarks and down quarks. Physicists sure have odd names for things! There are even quarks called "charm" and "strange."

One day, my dad came to Mr. Sell's class to show us some stuff about physics. He brought an aquarium tank and dry ice, which is frozen carbon dioxide gas. (How do you freeze a gas?) I looked around at my classmates, nervous as we watched him set up the tank on a table at the front of the classroom. Somehow, he used some rubbing alcohol and the dry ice to make a cloudy environment inside the tank.

When he finished, he told the class, "This is a cloud chamber. Come up close and take a look." We left our seats and crowded around the cloud chamber—an aquarium with a cloud inside!

"Here, Denise," he said, handing me a flashlight. "Shine this flashlight into the cloud and watch closely. Mr. Sell, can you please turn out the room lights?"

The room darkened. I turned on the flashlight and held it right up against the glass.

"Do you see any streaks through the cloud—lines of droplets?" he asked. We all peered into the cloud.

"Look, there's one!" I pointed and called out.

"Those are trails from tiny invisible pieces of matter," he told us.

Cosmic rays, which hit everything all the time, were making ions—tiny, charged pieces of matter—that were shooting through the cloud. "These tiny pieces of matter are too small to see. But you can see they exist because you can see the paths they leave behind," he explained.

I learned a lot in Mr. Sell's class and was especially interested in the science. But he influenced me the most by giving me Cs —he told my mom that I could do better than I was doing. That meant I had to work harder. Darn that Mr. Sell.

Flashlights & Typing

In high school in 1968, it was my turn to go up to the front of the classroom to meet with Mr. Riddle, my physics teacher. He was telling each of us, one by one, how we were doing in his class. I was one of only three girls in the class. I also was only one of three girls in my calculus class, but it was a different three girls. I guess I was the only one taking both classes.

"You're doing quite well for a girl," Mr. Riddle told me. "You understand the complicated terminology."

"Uh...okay...thanks," I replied and went back to my desk.

When I sat down, I nudged Martin, whose desk was next to mine. "Martin, Martin...guess what Mr. Riddle said," I whispered, leaning toward him. "He said I'm doing well... for a girl."

"Really? He said, 'for a girl'?"

"Yeah!" I said. "He really did!" We snickered. In 1968, when the National Organization for Women was lobbying for the Equal Rights Amendment, our generation was moving beyond the sex stereotypes. But Mr. Riddle clearly hadn't gotten the message. (I learned much later that more people hadn't gotten the message than I thought had.)

"A weirder thing," I said, "is that he told me I understand the complicated terminology. Well... we did have the word 'flashlight!'"

We broke up laughing. Mr. Riddle gave us a stare, and we toned it down to a snicker. But I told all my friends what Mr.

Riddle had said.

One day when I was a teenager, Dad was sitting with the newspaper in the living room, where I was reading a book, most likely science fiction.

"You know," he said, "You don't have to take typing. You're going to college."

I looked up from my book. "But they won't let me take it during the regular school year." My high school wouldn't let students in the college prep track take typing, so I had signed up to take it during the summer.

"If you can type, you may not have as many job options," he said.

At that time, in the 1960s, some people thought that if you were female, you shouldn't let anybody know you could type, because then you would always be supporting a boss—never to become a boss yourself.

"As a girl, you actually have more choices than if you were a boy," he continued.

"What do you mean? Why would I have more choices?"

"Well, women can choose a career or can choose to take care of a household. Men don't have that choice—men have to get a job and make a living so they can support a household. You have the freedom to have a career or not, to do whatever you want." He failed to mention that men had more choices than women for what career to pursue! And I guess he didn't realize that I could pay for college by typing—which I ended up doing by working at temp jobs typing on Magnetic Tape Selectric typewriters, the "word processors" of the day.

I don't think Dad wanted to be a househusband, but he did model egalitarian behaviors: he was the cook most of the time, and he would do things like vacuuming and laundry—things my friends' fathers would never do.

Though my mother didn't know how to use a hammer or

even how to change a battery, she did know how to count money, make work schedules, and handle a large crowd—she was the manager of a movie theater. And on television, Ann Sothern was always smarter than her boss, Gail Storm took charge of all the passengers on the cruises, and Lois Lane was brave and daring when trying to get her story (even though Superman had to save her). I watched their shows whenever I could; they were my role models.

So I saw a future where I would have a career. And since I was interested in science, I wanted to be a scientist like my father. When my parents' friends or our neighbors or even a teacher asked me what I was going to do after high school, I'd answer, "I'll go to college and then go into some type of science." But it took me another twenty years to discover the science I actually chose—the science of medicine and public health.

Studying Behavior

I t was registration day for my freshman year at college in 1969. It took me 15 minutes to walk across the campus from the commuter parking lot to the armory to register for classes at the University of Maryland in College Park. Founded in 1856 as an agricultural college, the university had become huge, with some 35,000 students, and a national leader in the sciences. Within commuting distance from where I lived with my parents and sisters, and with affordable in-state tuition. I never thought of going anywhere else. And, the icing on the cake, my boyfriend, Robert whom I later briefly married, was going there!

Throngs of incoming freshman filled the cavernous armory. They carried registration cards, stood in long lines, or sat on the floor going through course catalogs.

START HERE read a sign over a desk just inside the door.

"How does this work?" I asked the young woman sitting behind the desk.

"Here's a registration card," she told me. "Go to the table for the department teaching the class you want. Get the card initialed and your name written on the class roster to sign up. Here's a list of all the classes." She handed me a thick booklet.

I took the list of classes and my registration card over to the side of the room, sat down on the floor, leaned against the wall, and started going through the class list. What did I want to take? Differential calculus, physics, zoology, chemistry. Oh,

I need to take PE and a language—those are requirements. Six courses; a full schedule.

After hours of standing in lines for the various departments to sign me up, I was almost done. I had one slot still open because the chemistry class I wanted was full, so I would take it next semester. What should I take instead?

I stood in line for the College of Arts and Sciences. When I got to the front of the line, I asked, "What classes still have openings?"

"We have spots open in the Introduction to Psychology course," the young woman at the table told me.

The class was on a day and time that would fit well with my schedule. "I'll take it," I said. She initialed my card and put my name down on the class roster.

The psychology class was huge—over 200 students in a large lecture hall, and a closed-circuit TV in an overflow room.

When I signed up, I had no idea what psychology was. I learned that psychology is a science about behavior—why people and animals behave the way they do. Fascinated that you can study behavior as a science, I became a psychology major. Topics that interested me were those that linked biology with psychology—psychobiology or neuropsychology. Topics like why we perceive a picture as distorted even though our eyes are transmitting signals to our brains that are not distorted. Or studies of behaviors like the one of baby monkeys that could choose between a wire-cage "mother" that provided milk or a terry-cloth "mother" without milk. The baby monkeys stayed with the terry-cloth mother almost all the time—a comforting body seemed more important than food.

Behaviorism particularly fascinated me. Behaviorists don't study thoughts or feelings; what you can study, they say, is what you can observe. Thinking or feeling or motivations are in an unseen "black box." We can learn about behaviors by observing

PUBLIC HEALTH/PERSONAL DISEASE

animals without knowing what's in that box.

In a behaviorism course, we learned about Pavlov, who paired a bell with food for his dogs, who later salivated when hearing the bell even when there was no food—called classical conditioning. We also learned about B.F. Skinner, who posited that behaviors are shaped by their consequences, and rewards come after behaviors—called operant conditioning. I learned about "shaping" behaviors through positive reinforcement and not to reinforce unwanted behaviors. And I found out that learned behaviors are tough to change.

The course itself was designed to shape our behaviors as scientists. We did experiments with pigeons in Skinner boxes —where pigeons peck a key to open a seed cup. The instructors designed our first experiment and wrote our first laboratory report for us, with blanks where we filled in results of the experiment. For the next experiment, we had to make some decisions about the study design and use a report template that had less text pre-written and more blanks to fill in. We had to design the last experiment by ourselves and write it up with no help.

If we didn't like the score we got on a laboratory report, we could revise it. I even revised a report worth 60 points on which I got a 58; I just wanted to fix a couple of details. If we didn't like our grade on a test, we could retake it—the second time with different questions on the same topics. So this class was very much like the real scientific world, where if a journal rejects your paper, you can revise and resubmit it.

My experiments with my first pigeon went as expected. We were to alter the number and pattern of pecks needed to open the seed cup and observe what our pigeons did. I got the same results as Skinner, my classmates, and everybody else who had done the same experiments in every behaviorism class across the nation for years. When the same number of pecks was needed to open the seed cup every time (say 10 pecks each time), my pigeon would peck slowly at first and then speed up right before the seed cup opened. But when a different number of pecks caused the cup to open each time, so it was random and unpredictable—like maybe five pecks this time, one peck the next time, then 20 pecks a third time—my pigeon (like all the birds) pecked fast the whole time. It also took him longer to "extinguish" the learned behavior after the rewards stopped. And so I learned that intermittent positive reinforcement is powerful.

My second pigeon was a naïve pigeon that had never been in a Skinner box. I was supposed to train him to peck his button by "shaping" his behavior—rewarding him as he got closer and closer to his button until he pecked it. But whenever I put him in the Skinner box, he would go and stand next to his button, always in the same place with the button on his right at his eye level. Because of where he stood, turning his head was the only way he could get closer to his button. So, though I was supposed to train him to peck the button, he trained me to give him seed whenever he turned his head!

I had failed. I couldn't get pigeon number two to peck that darn button. So I cheated. I taped birdseed onto his button with clear tape so he could see it. Then when I put him in the box, he walked over to his button, noticed the seed taped onto it, and pecked at it. The seed cup opened, and he ate the seed. After I removed the tape, he pecked the bare button.

He was trained!

But he never stopped his head-turning behavior. I can see him right now in my mind's eye—jerking his head to the right, over and over again, hoping to get the seed cup to open, only occasionally pecking the button. Word spread about my strangely behaving pigeon, and some of my fellow students stopped by to see the bird I had trained to be neurotic. I wrote in my report what I had done, and my instructor wrote on my paper, "It's good to be honest."

I also took physics in college, especially because my father was a physicist. But I made the mistake of taking the advanced class, which used a lot of calculus. Calculus was invented by Sir Isaac Newton to explain the movement of objects, like the arc of a thrown ball and the orbit of the planets, so you can't do physics without calculus.

The course was hard for me. But I remember the "aha" moment when, magically, after about an hour of the professor showing step-by-step calculations on the chalkboard, the equation e = mc2 emerged! Energy equals mass times the speed of light squared. Mass and energy could be converted to each other! Cool! After that, I dropped physics—what else do you need to know? (I didn't tell my dad.)

Many years later, however, I read several physics books written for non-physicists. I wondered why there is a lack of epidemiology books for non-specialists. Epidemiology is the study of how diseases are distributed and what causes them in human populations—the scientific field I would end up pursuing but had yet to discover.

Frog Eggs

I knocked on the office door of the graduate student who was teaching the laboratory session of the embryology course I was taking in 1973. 'Ontogeny recapitulates phylogeny' read a sticker on his door. A semester earlier I wouldn't have known what that meant, but now I knew: Ontogeny is the development of an individual organism from conception to birth, and phylogeny is the evolution of organisms from one species to another, which created the animal phyla. So as an organism develops in utero or in an egg, it follows similar phases as evolution. That means humans have rudimentary gills during fetal development! Imagine that.

"Come in," said the teaching assistant. I opened the door and saw a messy office where a bearded, sandaled, jeaned young man leaned back on his chair with his feet propped up on his desk. "What can I do for you?"

"We're supposed to make up an experiment for class," I said. "Can I run an idea by you?"

"Sure. Go ahead."

"I read about how sperm fertilize eggs. I'm interested in the masked messenger hypothesis."

"Go on."

"I read that a coat of protein masks messenger RNA to keep it from replicating, and that fertilization might work by removing that coat."

"Yes, that's one hypothesis," he said.

"So what would happen if the protein coat was removed without sperm? Would eggs start developing as if they were fertilized?"

"Hmm…. Maybe. That's an interesting idea. It might make a good experiment."

"In class, you said we could get frog eggs for experiments. Could I use frog eggs to test this idea?"

"Hmmm… You could use an enzyme to break up protein, like trypsin," he replied. "I can look into getting you some."

"Wow. That would be great. So, how would we get the trypsin into the eggs?"

"Have you ever heated thin glass rods to pull them into fine needles?"

"No. Is it hard to do?"

"You may have to practice a bit. You have to be careful not to break the glass by pulling it too thin. You could dip the glass needles into some trypsin and stab the eggs with it."

"Cool. That sounds great."

"If you write up the rationale and design of the experiment, I'll look at it and see about getting you the materials. Don't forget to include a control group of eggs for comparison."

"Wow, this is great. Thanks so much!"

On the day of the experiment, my lab partner and I picked up our supplies: frog eggs, glass rods to heat up and pull into fine needles, a small vial of a clear liquid labeled "trypsin," and some incubation containers for the eggs.

Peering through a microscope that had eyepieces for both eyes (a stereoscopic microscope, with which I would later become intimately familiar), we pricked half the eggs with a glass needle dipped in the trypsin and the other half with a bare needle to serve as the control group. We couldn't see the protein coat, and we couldn't see the messenger RNA—but it was logical.

We put the eggs in two separate containers labeled "trypsin" and "control," and put the containers in the incubator. We'd come back in a few days to see the results.

Although we didn't get any actual frogs, twice as many of the eggs we pricked with trypsin started to develop compared with eggs we pricked with a bare needle. So the experiment was a success! I was excited to write up the findings in my paper for class, which I called "Artificial Parthenogenesis and the Masked Messenger Hypothesis." (Parthenogenesis is the reproduction of an egg without fertilization.)

One day, after listening to an embryology lecture, I got an idea for another experiment. I don't remember the specific idea, but I do remember going up to the professor after class and telling him about it.

"It's been done," he said, turning his back to me.

Dejected, I walked away, wondering what they had found when they did the experiment.

Despite this lack of encouragement, I ended up taking so many zoology courses that I had enough credits to graduate with a double major—psychology and zoology.

I thought about going to graduate school to study embryology. Maybe I could discover a birth control pill that men would use, instead of relying on women to take them—interested even then in the practical applications of science.

Embryology is part of zoology. But I was also interested in psychology. Is there a career that uses both fields?

Looking around at all the pre-med students in my classes (most of whom were men), it came to me—medicine! In medicine, you not only use both zoology and psychology, but you can help people!

When I told my parents I was thinking of going to medical school, my father arranged for me to meet a friend of his who had gone to medical school later in life. His friend told me that if I wanted to conduct research on people, medical school was the way to go.

So I took the Medical College Admissions Test (MCAT) and applied for admission to several highly ranked medical schools as well as the nearby state school—the University of Maryland at Baltimore. I was pleased to get into Maryland because it was nearby, it wasn't expensive, and it was the only school that accepted me.

Unlike most of my pre-med classmates whose fathers (and sometimes, but rarely, mothers) were doctors, and who had known for years they wanted to be a doctor, going to medical school didn't occur to me until my junior year in college. So I didn't know what to expect.

I didn't know that I would be beginning at least four, and as many as nine, years of training: two years of classroom study followed by two years of clinical training in medical school, then two to three years of a residency (the first year also called an internship), then possibly a subspecialty fellowship for a year or two or even three.

But going to medical school seemed like a good idea at the time.

SYMPTOMS

*I*t's a beautiful spring day in 2011. I'm walking across the campus of the National Institutes of Health to attend our institute's annual awards ceremony. I'm going because someone I nominated is getting an award.

The NIH campus is like a college campus, with multiple buildings, sidewalks, roads, and intersections with stop signs and pedestrian crosswalks. Today, the trees between the brick buildings are full of light-green spring leaves. Somewhere the NIH geese must be waddling, but I don't see them today.

I pause at a corner and wait for the cars to stop at the four-way stop signs. I cross the street and step up onto the sidewalk. I'm running late and need to get to the awards ceremony on time, so I'm walking fast. But the sidewalk is uneven, and my left foot catches on the pavement. I lose my balance.

Uh-oh. I'm falling. I can't stop myself. The concrete seems to rise to meet my face. I turn my head to the side, so I don't hit my nose. I put my right hand out to break the fall.

My right hand, right knee, and chin hit the pavement—hard.

Shit, I can't believe I fell! Did I say that out loud? "Shit! I can't believe I fell." This time I'm sure I say it out loud.

"Are you okay?" a woman leans over and asks me as I lie on the pavement. She must have been walking behind me.

"You should go to the employee health center," says another woman, after crossing the street to check on me.

Though shaken and hurt, I say, "I'm okay." They help me get up.

"It's just a little fall."

My knee bleeding, my hose torn, and my chin sore, I hobble to my destination a couple of buildings away. I enter the large auditorium and make my way up to the stage, where I'm supposed to sit for the awards ceremony with the other division directors. I choose a seat in the back of two rows to hide my bleeding knee.

As a master of ceremony calls out names, employees come up to the stage one by one or in a small group, and the institute director hands out award after award. As my employee climbs the stairs to get her award, I join her at the front of the stage for a photo. I hope my smile doesn't look as fake as it feels. I try to hide it, but I'm hurt and upset. I need to go home.

The exit door is on the other side of a reception area where snacks are set out—crackers and cheese, little chocolate muffins, punch. People greet me as I make my way through the crowd as I head for the exit door. "Congratulations. Congratulations," I say to award winners carrying their plaques.

A woman I know stops me and says, "What happened to you? Your knee is bleeding."

"I fell," I say. "I'm going home now."

"Do you need a ride?"

"I would love one—to my car. It's in the garage near my building," which is across the NIH campus. I drive home and ice my injuries.

It's March 2011. Barack Obama is president, the nation is in a financial slump, and American Idol is the number one TV program. I am the director of a division at the National Heart, Lung, and Blood Institute at NIH. And now my life will never be the same.

It's the day after I fell, and I'm going to see an orthopedist. I tell him about my fall. He examines me and takes x-rays.

"You have a small fracture in your right hand. We'll treat that with a removable splint. As for your knee, keep it clean, and it'll heal fine."

A couple of weeks later at a follow-up visit, I tell the orthopedist,

"My hand and knee are better. But I can't lift my left arm—the one without the fracture. It's stiff."

"Show me," he says.

I try to raise my arm but can't raise it above shoulder height. I try to reach behind my back, but can't. "It hurts," I say.

"You have a frozen shoulder," he says. "Here's a referral to physical therapy. Make an appointment on your way out."

The physical therapy center looks like a fitness center with exercise equipment everywhere: Exercise bicycles, treadmills, big colorful plastic exercise balls, hand weights, bands of rubber. In the center of the vast room amongst all the equipment are bench-tables that look like exam tables in a doctor's office. I guess they are for giving massages.

I meet Reena, my physical therapist. She is small—about five feet two—and a beauty of Middle Eastern origin.

Reena evaluates me then leads me through my first exercise. "Okay, first stand up," she says. "Now hinge forward at your waist and put your right hand on the bench. Now swing your left arm from the shoulder, back and forth, back and forth."

It doesn't swing very far. "It hurts."

"That's okay. It'll loosen up the more you do it. Now let's do a stretch. Stand up straight and bring your left arm across your body. Don't hunch up your shoulder. Good. Now with your right arm, gently pull your left elbow back toward your right shoulder. Relax into the stretch. Hold for 20 seconds."

We stand there while I stretch for one, two, three… nineteen, twenty.

"Good," she says. "Now let go of your arm, let it drop. Relax. Now repeat the stretch."

At a later session, she has me stand with my left side up against a wall and reach my left arm up along the wall until it hurts—and hold it. And she gives me an elastic band to do some shoulder exercises at home.

PT sessions twice a week for several weeks, and stretching twice a day at home, help to unfreeze my shoulder. But my left arm is still stiff and tensed up all the time. The word tetany comes to mind—a continuous steady contraction of a muscle.

My arm had gradually gotten stiffer over several weeks since my fall. I try to relax it, but it won't stay relaxed. And it doesn't swing when I walk. I try using a scarf as a sling, which helps me relax my arm, but it stiffens up again after removing the sling.

When I make a fist and tense up my left arm, it shakes. And I'm unable to make small movements with the fingers of my left hand. My right arm, in contrast, is relaxed, swings when I walk, and is as steady as a rock when I make a fist. And my right fingers are as nimble as ever.

My primary care doctor, Dr. Andrew asks, as all doctors do, "What brings you here today?" She usually checks my cholesterol and my blood pressure, gives me flu shots, and sends me to get mammograms. She's very good at the prevention aspect; now we'll see what happens when I have a problem.

I describe my fall, arm stiffness, and frozen shoulder. "I also am having difficulty with fine motor movements... see?" I show her that with my left hand I can't touch my thumb quickly to each finger one at a time; it gets stuck at the middle finger. I learned this test in medical school, and I've been testing myself.

"That's what worries me the most—the uncoordination," I tell her. "I'm dropping things, my typing has errors, and I'm having some trouble fastening necklaces. But it's only on the left."

Then I add, "And my left foot feels strange."

"Strange? What do you mean?" she asks.

"Well, sort of numb in the two smallest toes," I reply. "And my leg is achy, but not painful."

She looks puzzled. "Come up here on the exam table." She tests the strength in my arms and legs—they seem fine. She checks my reflexes and whether I can feel it when she touches my skin in various places

—everything seems normal.

"What could it be?" I ask. "Arthritis, MS, ALS…a brain tumor?"

She looks at me, nodding. "That's pretty much the list. Let's get you a brain MRI right away—today. And an MRI of your neck." She calls her nurse on the intercom who comes into the exam room and gives me an order form and instructions on where to get the MRIs.

A brain tumor is a definite possibility. Symptoms in my left arm and left leg could mean a tumor on the right side of my brain—because our brains control the opposite side of our bodies.

I get MRIs of my back, my neck, and my head. That same day I go to a physiatrist (a physical medicine doctor) who does an Electro-Myelogram and Nerve Conduction Study (EMG/NCS), which was ordered by the orthopedist. This test will find out how well my nerves are functioning from my neck down my left arm.

It was the same test my father had in his legs when he was diagnosed with ALS (Lou Gehrig's Disease)—a devastating disease that steals the ability to walk and later the ability to feed oneself, to swallow, and even to breathe. I took care of my dad during the year after his diagnosis—his last year of life. I'll never forget that year—it was twenty years ago now. I still miss him terribly.

When my husband, Bruce, comes home from work that evening, I say to him, "We need to talk." I take him by the hand and lead him over to the sofa. We sit down next to each other.

I look him in the eyes and say, "I've been having these symptoms, you know. I think I may have something serious. One thing I learned in my medical training is to recognize when symptoms could indicate a real problem."

"Oh, I'm sure you'll be fine," he said. "You're very healthy."

"Still, I think we should prepare ourselves mentally—just in case."

He holds my hand, and we just sit quietly without talking for several minutes.

PART 2: FROM MNEMONICS TO PATIENTS

"The good physician treats the disease; the great physician treats the patient who has the disease."

—William Osler

Information Overload

I n 1974, before the Inner Harbor in Baltimore was turned into a tourist destination—when there was so much trash on the water that it looked like you could walk on it— I moved to Baltimore to attend the University of Maryland School of Medicine, the nation's oldest public medical school. When the school was founded in 1807, numerous infectious diseases plagued Baltimore, and the average life expectancy was 34 years. History has it that the medical faculty would rob cemeteries to get corpses for studying anatomy. Indeed, in the bowels of Davidge Hall there still was a corpse, partially dissected, hard as a rock, for us medical students to discover.

All 200 of us medical students in the Class of 1978—a quarter of us female (the highest proportion ever)—took the same courses. While the Vietnam War ended and the Supreme Court ruled on the Roe v Wade case that legalized abortion, we were busy memorizing facts. You name it; we memorized it. Anatomy, physiology, histology, microbiology, pathology, pharmacology. Parts of the skeletal system, the nervous system, the gastrointestinal system, the cardiovascular system. How body systems function, disease processes, treatments.

It was information overload. How were we possibly going to keep all this information in our heads? Why by mnemonics of course!

Many people are familiar with this mnemonic: "My Very Educated Mother Just Served Us Nine Pickles"—the first letter of each word stands for one of the planets, from the sun outward: Mercury, Venus, Earth, Mars, Jupiter, Saturn, Uranus, Neptune, Pluto. They probably have dropped Pluto now that it's considered a dwarf planet—one of many natural satellites in the Kuiper belt. Perhaps now the mnemonic is: "My Very Educated Mother Just Served Us Nothing."

Here's a mnemonic for the cranial nerves, also called bulbar nerves—twelve nerves that come directly out of our brains—in the order they exit the brain from top to bottom: "On Old Olympus' Towering Top, A Finn And German Vault And Hop." Each word stands for one of the nerves: Olfactory, Optic, Oculomotor, Trochlear, Trigeminal, Abducens, Facial, Auditory, Glossopharyngeal, Vagus, Accessory, and Hypoglossal. I admit I didn't remember the nerves and had to look them up as I wrote this—I remembered the mnemonic, but not the nerves. (There are several dirty ones also, mostly sexist, such as, "Oh, Oh, Oh, To Touch And Feel A Great Vagina. Ah Happy!")

If a mnemonic didn't already exist, we made one up. A lot of people make them up. A website today called medicalmnemonics.com has 52 mnemonics just for the anatomy of the skeletal system!

Most of the professors imparted information through lectures that weren't very dynamic or engaging and were held in a darkened lecture hall back when we thought slides needed to have white letters on a dark background. Many of us fell asleep during class.

So an enterprising student named Stuart organized a note-taking service. Student volunteers attended class and took notes, and the rest of us paid for a photocopy—a fuzzy, hard to read photocopy, but a summary of the lecture nonetheless. Faculty knew about the note-taking service—they probably had one also when they were medical students.

The first year, Stuart let anybody be a note-taker. But the ability to take clear and readable notes varied dramatically, so the second year Stuart selected the best note-takers, and he paid them something from fees he charged the rest of us for copies.

Probably only a third of the students went to class, and that was for the good lecturers! A picture in the yearbook (surely staged) shows a professor lecturing to a sole student in our huge lecture hall, with the caption "the Stuart Memorial Lecture." We joked that the next step would be the professor audiotaping his lecture, and then playing it to another tape recorder that would record it for the students—there would be just the two tape recorders in the lecture hall, "talking" to each other!

We had frequent exams—very often on Mondays, pretty much ruining our weekend social lives. The faculty posted our scores on a bulletin board using our ID numbers (no names) for confidentiality. The scores were in descending order, so we could see what grade we got as well as where we were in relation to our classmates.

All 200 of us had been at the highest end of the grade distributions, the best scores in our classes, our entire lives—that's how we got into medical school. But now that we all were in this highly selected group called "medical students," somebody had to be at the bottom. Some students were devastated when they saw their scores at the bottom of the list. But everything came out fine, because, as the joke goes: "What do they call the medical school graduate who ranks lowest in his class?" Answer: "Doctor."

Medical school was overwhelming. It also wasn't very interesting to me. Was I wrong in thinking that medicine was based on science? They weren't teaching us science; they were teaching us facts—scientific facts, yes, but nothing about how people discovered the facts. No experiments described, like the dual-slit experiment in physics where electrons were shown to be both particles and waves.

I slept late a lot and skipped a lot of classes. When I did go to class, I would sit in the back and sometimes slip out with a friend—maybe with my boyfriend, Jerry, to go to the zoo. Jerry was sweet, kind, Jewish, handsome, dark with a thick mustache, and one of the smartest people I've ever known. At one point, we lived together and talked about getting married.

I got the notes from the note-taking service, and I read the textbook, so I guess I was using a more flexible, though not officially sanctioned, form of education.

I was a fair to middling student, doing fine on the tests, generally right in the middle of the grade distribution. But I wondered what I had signed up for. And I completely forgot about my interest in science—I was busy memorizing vast amounts of information.

The medical school was driving distance from my parents' house, so I would try to go home for Sunday dinners.

One Sunday, I told Dad about skipping classes. He frowned and said, "One day a patient will come to see you who has a problem with his leg, and you'll have to say, 'I'm sorry, but I didn't go to class the day they taught about legs.'"

I replied that I would refer the patient to someone else.

A bit later, after I got a stethoscope, I would lie in the dark and listen to my own heart, trying to visualize the valves opening and closing, which is what makes that lub-dub sound.

And I was taught how to peer into someone's eyes and see the optic nerve where the blood vessels and nerves enter the eye's retina. And I got to see someone's vocal cords, using a little mirror on a bent stick, a light, and holding the patient's tongue out—the two white sides of the vocal cord coming together as the patient said "eee." Cool.

So it might be more interesting and motivating when I got to the clinical years—the third and fourth years of medical school. At least that's what I hoped at the time.

I Wasn't Ready

"C'mon gang, let's get crackin.' It's time for rounds," said the resident, Dr. Modell, our hospital team leader. "We have loads of patients to talk about." He pulled the wheeled metal file of patient charts out from under the counter at the nurses' station and rolled it down the gray tiled hallway of University Hospital. We may not need the files, but he wanted them handy in case we needed to look up a test result.

It was 1976, my third year of medical school, and I was starting my first clinical rotation—hands-on training where you "rotate" through various disciplines a month at a time.

Here at University Hospital—and over the next two years at other hospitals affiliated with the University of Maryland—I learned how to read a medical chart, do a urinalysis, give a shot, draw blood, and do "scut work" like going to the laboratory to get test results. I also learned that sometimes patients are riddled with cancer and beyond treatment, sweet old ladies can die when they follow medical advice, and babies can get hopelessly sick and die for no apparent reason.

Dr. Modell was thin with black hair, dark-rimmed glasses, and a mustache. He was a typical team leader at a teaching hospital at the time: A white male who had gone through four years of pre-med in college and four years of medical school, followed by two years of residency (the first year also called an internship) and now in his third, and often last, year of residency. After this year, he could join a medical practice—unless he was going to go into a sub-specialty, like neurology, in which case he'd do a fellowship for another year or two.

Five of us were on the medical team for the internal medicine service: Dr. Modell, one intern, one fourth-year medical student, and two third-year medical students. Wearing a crisp new white jacket, my new stethoscope in my pocket, holding a notepad and pencil, I was one of those third-year students.

The intern followed Dr. Modell down the hall, making it clear he was next in the pecking order. A licensed doctor himself, he had just passed the state medical board examination after graduating from medical school.

The fourth-year medical student followed behind, visibly excited—maybe because she was almost finished with medical school, she now could choose her rotations, or perhaps she was a 'hot dog' eager to make a good impression.

We third-year medical students straggled after them.

Standing in the corridor, our team talked about the patients: their medical histories, symptoms, diagnoses, pathology, test results, treatment plan, and progress. I wrote down words I didn't know so I could look them up later, because, as I was learning, a lot of medicine is vocabulary.

"Our first patient today is Mrs. Glass," Dr. Modell said as we approached her room. "She has heart failure. Her symptoms are *dyspnea* [shortness of breath], *nocturia* [getting up to urinate during the night], *orthopnea* [difficulty breathing while lying down], and peripheral *edema* [legs swollen with fluid]."

We followed Dr. Modell into the room toward the bedside of a pale elderly white woman with white hair, folds of skin surrounding her wrinkled face. She wore a pink quilted bed-jacket.

The head of her hospital bed was raised to a 45-degree angle. Her breakfast, partially eaten, sat on the wheeled bedside table.

Dr. Modell patted her on the forearm and said, "Good morning, dear. How are you feeling today?"

"I'm doing better," she replied, smiling.

"Let's see how your legs are doing." He pulled back the covers to expose her feet and felt her swollen ankles. "How's your breathing when you lie down?"

"It's better, doctor."

He put his stethoscope into his ears and listened to her heart (front of chest) and lungs (back of chest). "All of you, get your stethoscopes out and come listen to Mrs. Glass's heart. Check out her ankles too—see the edema?"

Turning to Mrs. Glass, he asked, "You don't mind, dear, do you?"

"Of course not, doctor," she said, gazing at him with admiration.

We took turns listening to her heart. I heard the 'whoosh whoosh' of a heart murmur caused by turbulent blood flow through an abnormal heart valve.

When we were finished listening to her heart, Mrs. Glass smiled and said, "Thank you. I'm glad you find my heart interesting."

Some of us waved goodbye as we filed out of the room.

"Do any of you know why heart failure gives you the symptoms that Mrs. Glass has?" our resident asked us when we were in the hallway again.

The fourth-year student spoke up: "The heart doesn't function right, maybe because the heart muscle is weak, or maybe a heart valve doesn't close all the way. So blood backs up from the heart into the lung veins."

"Right," said the resident. "But why is that a problem?"

The intern added: "Increased pressure in the veins causes fluid to seep out through the vein walls. Fluid fills the *alveoli*." [Tiny sacs in our lungs where oxygen enters, and carbon dioxide leaves the bloodstream.]

"Yes. Vein walls are more like canvas tent walls than like plastic—they can leak."

Mrs. Glass had reported she had rheumatic fever as a teenager. Strep throat, if not treated, can cause rheumatic heart disease. When the body makes antibodies against the strep germs, those antibodies can attack body cells instead of just the germs. They can attack heart valves, which causes rheumatic heart disease and subsequent heart failure.

"Her heart failure can be treated but not cured. Mrs. Glass is being treated and is almost ready to go home," Dr. Modell said.

"Our next patient is Mr. Bud," he said as we moved down the hallway. "He came to the Emergency Room last night vomiting blood. Mr. Bud is assigned to our intern."

The intern told us that Mr. Bud was a long-time alcoholic. He had cirrhosis of the liver—a chronic condition where liver tissue thickens and so blood couldn't flow easily from the gastrointestinal tract into the liver, causing excess pressure in the *portal veins* (veins going from the intestines to the liver). Blood in the portal veins backed up, causing the blood vessels inside the bottom of the esophagus to swell (called esophageal *varices*). The varices had burst—a life-threatening condition, which caused the bleeding Mr. Bud had vomited up.

"The ER doc put a plastic tube down his esophagus and blew up a balloon at the end of the tube to press on the esophageal varices," the intern told us. "The bleeding stopped. He's dehydrated, so we put in an IV."

"Alcoholism is a model disease for understanding how the liver connects to the GI system," Dr. Modell told us. "But it's a horrible thing to see people do to themselves. We'll try to talk him into going into rehab, but his prognosis is grim. Let's go see him."

A middle-aged male patient with darkish skin and black hair —perhaps Hispanic or Italian or middle-eastern—Mr. Bud was lying in bed on his left side with his back to us. An IV bag hung on a pole, its tube leading into his right arm, which extended across his body, where he was holding onto the raised left-sided bed railing.

"Mr. Bud? Mr. Bud?" Dr. Modell tried to get his attention, but he didn't move. We heard him snoring. "Let's let him rest." We went back out to the hallway.

"Our next patient is the Crater Lady," Dr. Modell said, moving to the next doorway. "She has a large decubitus ulcer. I didn't assign her to anybody because we're just feeding her by a stomach tube to get her nutrition in better shape. Once her blood albumin improves, we'll turf her to surgery." (A *decubitus ulcer* is an open wound on the skin caused by pressure, like lying in bed without moving for hours. *Serum albumin* is a protein in blood, which can help indicate nutritional status. Turf is not actually a medical term.)

"Let's check her latest albumin result." He pulled her chart out of the rolling cart of patient charts, opened it, and said, "Nope. Still not good enough."

The fourth-year student spoke up. "Why do you call her the Crater Lady?" she asked.

"The ulcer is so big that it's like a crater. You can put your whole fist into it."

Ugh, I thought. How awful. I just had to say something. "How did that happen?"

"She stopped walking years ago. They couldn't figure out why. And whoever took care of her didn't do a good job. We don't need to see her today. Let's move on."

And on we went—patient after patient, ad nauseum, for two more hours.

It was hard for me to stand for that long. I shifted my weight to one foot, then to the other foot. I put my pencil back into my pocket, looked at my watch, and leaned against the wall. I closed my eyes. I fell asleep! Then I woke myself up, shifted my weight to the other foot, took my pencil out, and tried to pay attention.

Everybody on the team had to present patients to the group. When the intern presented his patients, he was concise, often talked rapidly, and knew essential pieces of information by heart including what they meant.

The fourth-year student generally took a little longer to present her patients, sometimes looking at her notes, sometimes being a "hot dog" spewing out facts, perhaps having stayed up late to read about the disease.

As an average third-year student, when I presented a patient, I referred to my notebook where I had written down the patient's information, and I mentioned every detail, not knowing what was important and what wasn't. Other team members would shift their weight from one foot to the other, look at their watches, lean against the wall, and sometimes close their eyes.

My First Patient

"You'll have only one patient to start. His name is Mr. Harris," Dr. Modell told me, leaning forward so we could hear each other among the commotion of activity at the fifth-floor nurse's station. "Read his chart and go see him, and we'll talk about him when you're done. I'll give you more patients later." Then he added, "Mr. Harris should be easy; he's just here to die."

"What do you mean, he's just here to die?"

"He's got cancer," Dr. Modell explained. "It probably started in his lungs. It's all over his body now and in his bones. He's 'no CPR' and on pain meds. Go see him. If he's in any discomfort tell me, and we can increase the pain meds. And write a SOAP note on the chart."

"A SOAP note?" I asked.

"Oh, sorry. I forgot this is your first rotation. SOAP is an acronym for Subjective, Objective, Assessment, and Plan—Subjective is the symptoms, what the patient feels and reports; Objective is what you find on a physical or tests; Assessment is your evaluation; Plan is what's going to be done, like tests or treatments. It's a standard way to write a progress note."

I located Mr. Harris's chart at the nurses' station. The metal-covered chart contained pages and pages of doctors' and nurses'

notes, laboratory results, and reports about x-rays and other tests—not just from this hospital admission, but also from probably about a dozen hospitalizations over 40 years.

In the notoriously bad handwriting of a physician, I found the following admission note from about a week ago:

"70 yo WM from LMD, Dx metastatic Ca x 5 mos, cause unknown (likely lung). 80 pack-yr smoker. Wt loss x 1 year. CXR lesions in lungs, bone. Pt c/o pain. Oriented x 3. Admit. Pain mngmt. No code."

It took me about 15 minutes, but finally, I worked out what it meant—simultaneously learning that a lot of medicine is not only vocabulary but is also abbreviations:

The patient is a 70-year old white male, sent to the hospital by a local M.D. He was diagnosed with metastatic cancer five months ago. The cause of the cancer is unknown but is likely from his lungs. He smoked 80 pack-years (for example, two packs a day for 40 years). He's been losing weight for about four months. His chest X-ray shows lesions in his lungs and bones. The patient complains of pain. He's oriented to person, place, and time (he knows who people are, where he is, and what day it is). Admit him to the hospital for pain management. As per family wishes, if his heart stops, don't do CPR or give an electric shock to start it up again—just let him die.

The chart noted that the cause was unknown because they hadn't confirmed the source of the cancer was his lungs. The family had refused a biopsy because it was unnecessary and would be painful, and it was clear that the cancer had spread all over his body.

A decade earlier, a Surgeon General's landmark report had concluded that smoking causes lung cancer. Mr. Harris's 80 pack-years of smoking were clearly to blame.

In 1976 when I saw Mr. Harris, 37 percent of adults smoked. Today it's much lower, about 17 percent—the message of harm widely known.

The door to Mr. Harris's room was ajar. Knocking lightly on the doorjamb, I entered. First, I noticed the room smelled like body odor. I felt a bit queasy. Next, I noticed roses in a vase on the bedside table, drooping their heads over a glass of false teeth in water. Then I saw Mr. Harris, lying on his back in bed, his face turned away from me, staring out the window. I could just make out the outline of his small body under the white hospital blanket. His thin hair was almost completely gone, and his skin was sallow and frail.

"Hello," I said. "I'm one of the medical students."

He turned his head and looked at me. "Hi," he said, grinning a weak toothless grin.

"I'll be checking on you every day to see how you're doing. How do you feel today? Are you in any pain?"

"I feel okay, I guess." His voice was soft, his speech slow. "I'm about as comfortable as I can be, I guess." He turned his head away to stare out the window again.

"Do you know where you are, what day it is, why you're here?"

"Sure," he said, looking back at me. "Everybody asks me that, so I keep track. It's Monday and I'm in University Hospital." He was lucid and oriented. He paused, and then he said, "I have cancer." I could barely hear him.

I wrote a SOAP note on the chart: S—not in pain; O—oriented and lucid; emaciated; A—diagnosis of terminal metastatic cancer; P—make him comfortable, no code.

Later Dr. Modell told me to go to the Radiology Department and look at Mr. Harris's chest x-ray. He said it was amazing because you can see only half the clavicle; the bone had been eaten away by the cancer.

When I entered Mr. Harris's room the next morning, the roses were gone. The false teeth, still in their glass of water on the night table, greeted me with a toothy grin. Mr. Harris was still in bed. He didn't greet me at all.

A woman with gray hair pulled into a bun at the nape of her neck sat erect in the visitor's chair, her back to me as I entered. She was watching Mr. Harris.

"Excuse me," I said.

She turned to look at me. "Hi," she said.

"Hi," I said. "I have to check on him today, but I can come back later if you'd like."

"It's okay. You can see him now. I'm his sister. I was just visiting."

Moving to stand next to the bed, I said, "Good morning, Mr. Harris." He didn't respond. He was staring out the window.

I put my hand on his shoulder. He looked up at me. "Good morning, Mr. Harris," I repeated, more loudly this time. "How are you today?"

He answered, but his answer was gibberish. He turned his head to stare out the window again. I looked at his sister. Her eyes were wet.

Later that day, I asked the resident what had happened. He told me that the cancer had most likely spread to Mr. Harris's brain.

"But in only one day?" I asked. "He was lucid yesterday."

"It happens," he said.

Mr. Harris was lying in bed the next morning, staring out the window as usual. The toothy grin was still in its watery grave on the bedside table. His sister was sitting again, or maybe all along, in her chair between the bed and the doorway.

I moved to stand next to her chair. "We're giving him pain medication," I said to her. "So he's not in any pain."

She looked up at me. "How do you know?" she asked.

She was right. I didn't really know. He just didn't look like he was in pain.

I probably should have moved on to see other patients that I had now, but I started talking with Mr. Harris's sister.

Although everybody else was talking about Watergate, President Ford, and the Vietnam War, those were not topics on her mind. Her brother and cancer were the only topics on her mind.

"My brother has lived with me for ten years—since my husband died," she said. "Now my neighborhood is run down—it's not safe to walk down the street anymore, not like it was when I moved in. I pray every day he'll get better and come back home. I feel safer when he's there. I could take care of him—why does he need to be here, in the hospital?"

Today I would have said that he doesn't need to be in the hospital—that he could get hospice care so he could die at home. But I couldn't say it then. Legislation for federal funding of hospice programs had been introduced in 1974 but hadn't passed. Nursing home beds were scarce, and so hospitals were logical places for people to die.

I talked with Mr. Harris's sister for over an hour, mostly about our hope that a cure for cancer would someday be discovered.

All while Mr. Harris stared out the window.

The next morning when I went back to Mr. Harris's room the bed was bare, the room devoid of personal objects. There were no false teeth on the bedside table to greet me; no woman was sitting in a chair between the bed and the door. Mr. Harris was not there. I confirmed at the nurse's station that he had died during the night, alone.

Walking through the hospital lobby about an hour later, I saw Mr. Harris's sister. I walked up to her.

"Did you hear?" she asked. "I was home, and they called me."

"Yes," I said. "I heard." I wanted to say more, but she turned and walked away.

Later, while attending a lecture on some disease or another, I recalled the sister's face. I might have imagined it, but I think she had looked relieved.

I never did go see that x-ray. I did, however, go home that night and cry.

Sutton's Law

"**D**enise, my girl," Dr. Woodward stared straight at me from where he stood in front of the classroom. A middle-aged, intense man with gray hair who wore his glasses halfway down his nose, he leaned forward on his hands spread out in front of him on a wooden table. "Denise, my girl, what's Sutton's Law?"

I always felt so inadequate when he called on me. I hardly ever knew the answer. And if I did know an answer, he would keep asking questions until he got to one that I didn't know. He did that to all the students. There was always a point where the student didn't know as much as Dr. Woodward, the Chief of Medicine, knew.

"Sutton's law?" I asked. "Uh..."

About 20 of us third-year medical students were in a classroom for a didactic session where Dr. Woodward was employing his version of the Socratic method. He didn't give me a chance to think. He looked around the room, rested his eyes on Joe, and asked, "Joe, my boy, who was Willie Sutton?"

"I don't know, sir," Joe answered.

"Boys and girls, Willie Sutton!" He slapped his hand on the table. "You don't know who Willie Sutton was?"

He paused, "He was a bank robber, kids."

Looking around the room, he said, "'You're probably wondering what a bank robber has to do with anything. Do you know what Willie Sutton said when asked why he robbed banks?"

Leaning forward again, his hands back on the table, Dr. Woodward paused. We squirmed.

"He said, 'That's where the money is.' Remember that, kids. Follow Sutton's Law and go where the money is. And don't go thinkin' that I'm talkin' about how much you'll make!"

He paced back and forth.

I hope he doesn't call on me again, I thought. *Maybe I shouldn't look at him.*

Then he walked over to a lightbox where an x-ray film was mounted. He turned on the light. "What's this patient got right there? Right there in the apex of his lung?" he asked, pointing to the top of the left lung on the x-ray.

"Come on, kids, what's he got? You know he's got something —it's all hazy there. That's where the money is, boys and girls. What's he got? He's been coughing. He has a fever. He wakes up with night sweats. He's been losing weight. What's he got? Joe, what do you think?"

Joe stammered, "Uh…Can we do some tests? Can we look at his sputum?"

"Good idea, son!" Dr. Woodward said, punching the air with his fist. "Let's look at his sputum! That's where the money is. So we looked at his sputum under a microscope, and what did we find? Denise, my girl, what do you think this patient has?"

He looked straight at me again. "Idiopathic pulmonary fibrosis?" I guessed.

"We found acid-fast bacilli, boys and girls." He slapped his palm on the table and looked around the room. "Tubercle bacilli." He looked right at me. "He had tuberculosis! Just like you said!"

"Boys and girls, when you hear hoofbeats behind you, would you expect to see a zebra or a horse? Why a horse—because it's more common! This patient's symptoms and x-ray are textbook TB. Only go looking for zebras if you can't find a horse."

A couple of weeks later, my supervising resident asked me to present a case to the students at one of Dr. Woodward's sessions—a 92-year-old woman who had a "silent myocardial infarction." The only symptom she had for her heart attack was vomiting; she didn't have any chest pain.

I began: "This 92-year old woman, admitted to the hospital for..."

Dr. Woodward stopped me mid-sentence. Peering at me, he said, "Wait...she was how old?" He seemed shocked at the advanced age, unusual in the 1970s.

Many years later when I was responsible for a study that tested a community-wide program to help people identify heart attack symptoms and seek care for them, I remembered my elderly patient whose only symptom of a heart attack was vomiting.

Dr. Woodward died in 2005 at the age of 91, and stories of Willie Sutton, hoofbeats, and zebras continue to be handed down to this day.

Ten Pounds

Paul and I were two medical students doing an internal medicine rotation in 1977, when the medical resident, Dr. Jones, saw Mr. Burch in the Emergency Department while we watched. He asked the patient why he had come to the hospital.

Mr. Burch said, "I'm short of breath. It's my lungs."

"How far can you walk without having to stop and catch your breath?" asked Dr. Jones.

"I can barely walk across a room."

"How many pillows do you sleep on?"

"Well, three."

"What happens if you lie down flat?"

"Then I can't breathe," Mr. Burch said. "Can you help me?

"I need to ask a few more questions. Do you get up at night to urinate?"

"I get up about three times a night to pee."

"Have you gained any weight?"

"Yeah, I've gained a ten pounds in the past month."

The doctor listened to the patient's lungs and told him, "I'm admitting you to the ICU for heart failure."

"Heart failure? I didn't know I had a heart problem! I thought it was my lungs."

"Your heart can affect your lungs," Dr. Jones explained to the patient. "We'll be right back." He led Paul and me out of the examining room for a teachable moment.

In the hallway, Dr. Jones asked us, "So how would you describe this patient's symptoms?"

Remembering teaching rounds and my vocabulary list, I said, "He has dyspnea, orthopnea, and nocturia."

"Correct," said Dr. Jones. "And his blood gasses show a low level of oxygen and a high level of carbon dioxide." The air exchange in the alveoli wasn't occurring. It was like he was drowning.

"So what treatment do you think we should give him?" he asked us.

"Diuretics and digitalis just like in Dr. Woodward's story," said Paul. "Diuretics will get rid of the extra fluid. Digitalis will make his heart contract more strongly."

"Ah, so you've heard Dr. Woodward's stories, have you?" Said Dr. Jones. "Always remember Dr. Woodward's stories."

Dr. Woodward had told us that if you are a new doctor in town, and a patient comes to you with trouble breathing because of fluid in his lungs from acute heart failure, you should call up a Boy Scout. Have the Boy Scout by your side when you treat the patient. You can improve the patient's condition in short order by giving diuretics and digitalis. The Boy Scout will then run around town telling everybody what a great doctor you are. Everybody believes a Boy Scout.

So Dr. Jones ordered diuretics and digitalis, just like in Dr. Woodward's story. He also ordered oxygen because Mr. Burch's blood oxygen level was low.

"I have a job for you two," Dr. Jones told Paul and me. "I'm worried Mr. Burch will get worse if he falls asleep and doesn't keep breathing deeply. I want you to keep him awake all night and make sure he takes deep breaths."

So we followed Mr. Burch as he was wheeled on a gurney from the Emergency Department to the ICU. And we stayed up all night at his bedside.

He kept falling asleep, so we woke him up. "Wake up and breathe, breathe," one of us would say. He took a couple of deep breaths and slipped off to sleep again. Shaking his shoulder or tapping his arm, the other of us would say, "Wake up! You need to breathe. Breathe deeply."

"But I'm so tired."

"Sorry—doctor's orders."

We did this all night long. By morning, Mr. Burch was much better. He had lost a lot of the excess fluid from his lungs and was breathing comfortably. He was moved out of the ICU to a bed on the regular floor.

He went home in three days, his heart failure under control on a new medication regimen. But I wondered if Dr. Jones had just wanted us to be there all night because no Boy Scouts were available!

Several years later, my grandmother, Sittee, who had a "leaky valve" from rheumatic heart disease, just like Mr. Burch, was admitted to the hospital for an episode of acute heart failure, which she had intermittently suffered from for decades. When I went to visit her, her doctor took me aside and said, "I want to let you know that we are treating her with digitalis and trying to reduce the fluid in her lungs. But, because of her advanced age, her kidneys aren't responding to the diuretics. Her condition is life threatening."

This was the last hospital visit for Sittee—my grandmother who taught us to sing and how to make baklava and to roll grape leaves, and that fish aren't animals.

Only about a year after Sittee passed away, the results of the DIG (pronounced with a soft Gee) trial were released. *Digitalis Reduces Hospitalization for Heart Failure,* read the title of the 1997 press release from the National Heart, Lung, and Blood Institute, where I worked at the time. But the first sentence was the kicker: "Digitalis, one of the most commonly used heart drugs, has no effect on survival of heart failure patients."

The DIG trial, which studied 6,700 patients with heart failure, had found no difference in mortality rates between heart failure patients randomly assigned to receive digitalis or to receive a placebo dummy pill. Though the press release had played up a positive finding (something I learned later was fairly common), you really couldn't find a more negative study. Mortality, the primary outcome, was identical in the two randomized groups: on a graph, the lines showing accumulating deaths over time in the treatment and placebo groups lay on top of each other.

As early as ancient Rome, digitalis, derived from the foxglove plant, had been used to treat various conditions. After it was purified into digoxin in the late 1700s, doctors used it to treat heart failure. The drug increases the strength of heart muscle contractions, and it seemed logical that increasing heart contractility would improve heart failure outcomes. So the DIG results in 1997 made big news because a commonly used and trusted medicine was found not to prevent deaths as had been logically assumed for hundreds of years.

DIG is an example of a frequently used treatment that was used for decades without being rigorously tested for its effects on health outcomes. Researchers have estimated that only about 10% of clinical recommendations in cardiology, for example, are based on evidence from randomized trials—which provide the highest quality of evidence in medicine.

A lot of the practice of medicine is based on logic, not on evidence.

Boom, That'll Be It!

Moving to another hospital for another internal medicine rotation as a medical student, I was assigned to Mrs. Pigeon. A gray-haired elderly woman always with a smile on her face, Mrs. Pigeon was a sweetheart, friendly to everybody.

She was admitted to the hospital with a urinary tract infection that needed IV antibiotics. Upon admission, the hospital had taken a routine chest x-ray—standard practice for every patient admitted to the hospital, whether or not they had lung symptoms, history of smoking, or family history of lung cancer.

Today routine chest x-rays, taken for no specific reason, have limited evidence of their usefulness, but they were common—routine, in fact—in the 1970s.

The radiologist who read the x-ray saw a shadow that looked suspicious. He recommended getting an ultrasound. That's when they found an aortic aneurysm.

The aorta is the huge artery that rises out of the heart, then bends backward and goes down behind the heart. Branches go off to the arms, and the aorta keeps going down through the abdomen, dividing in two to create the large femoral arteries that go down the legs. Sometimes part of the aorta wall is weak and bulges out like a balloon—that's an aneurysm.

A consulting surgeon had told Mrs. Pigeon that one day her aorta would burst, and she would die. She could just be walking down the street and "boom, that will be it."

Mrs. Pigeon was justifiably scared. She agreed to have surgery to repair her aorta.

A resident I knew, we'll call Dr. Adams, had just left internal medicine to do a rotation in pathology. He stopped by to see me, to talk with me about Mrs. Pigeon's pending surgery.

"Don't let them operate on that sweet little old lady. She doesn't need it. She has no symptoms—why put her through all that? Just let her be."

Maybe he was right, but Mrs. Pigeon had agreed to have the surgery; the surgeon had scared her into it. (Some people would say that a surgeons' motto was "when in doubt, cut it out.") But nobody explained to me how they knew this aortic aneurism needed an operation. Was it based on the aneurism's size? On its location? On the patient's age? I admit I didn't ask. What difference would it make anyway? It had been decided that Mrs. Pigeon would have the surgery.

Here's a SOAP note I could have written on Mrs. Pigeon's chart: 'Subjective—sweet old lady with no symptoms; Objective—aortic aneurysm on ultrasound; Assessment—possibly needs surgery; surgeon thinks so; Plan—surgery, just in case.'

The day before Mrs. Pigeon's surgery, I pulled a chair up to her bedside and sat down. Leaning toward her, I asked her how she was doing. This was the first time I had seen her without a smile on her face.

"I'm worried," she said.

"It'll be okay," I replied. "The surgeon is very good."

"That's not what's bothering me," she said, looking down and picking at her blanket. "I have a grown daughter I haven't seen in years. I've never even seen my two grandchildren."

I didn't ask what had happened—she didn't need to tell me. The important point was that she was estranged from her daughter and grandchildren. Now that she was having risky surgery, shouldn't her daughter know?

"Do you want me to call your daughter and tell her about the surgery?" I asked.

She looked up at me, her eyes lit up. "You'd do that for me? That'd be so kind. Please tell her. And tell her I wanna see her. She doesn't live very far away."

So that afternoon, I looked up Mrs. Pigeon's next-of-kin information and, sure enough, it included her daughter's phone number and address—only about five miles away. I called the daughter from the nurses' station and told her about the surgery scheduled for the next day.

"It's major surgery—and risky," I said. "But the surgeon thinks she needs it, and she wants to have it done. She wants to see you."

"I'll come see her tonight, before the surgery," the daughter said. "Thank you so much for calling me."

I hung up and went to tell Mrs. Pigeon before going home that night.

The next morning I ran into Dr. Adams in the cafeteria. "I saw your patient this morning," he told me, staring directly into my eyes. Though I don't remember what Dr. Adams looked like, or even his real name, I'll never forget that moment.

"You did? Really?" I asked, surprised. How could he have seen my patient?

He just looked at me and waited until I figured it out. He was doing a pathology rotation! Oh my god, she must have died during surgery that morning. He had seen her in the morgue!

"No!" I said.

"Yes," he replied.

I had to check this out myself! I ran up the stairs and down the hall to Mrs. Pigeon's room. A nurse was getting the room ready for its next occupant.

"What happened?" I asked.

The nurse turned toward me and said, "Mrs. Pigeon died on the operating table at 7 o'clock this morning."

"Oh no!" I said. "Well, at least her daughter came see her last night."

"I'm afraid not," she replied. "The daughter never showed up."

I got lightheaded and had to sit down. I imagined Mrs. Pigeon, awake all night, waiting for a daughter who never came.

God's Thumb

First, the resident, and then the Emergency Department doctor had examined LaVonda, a nine-month-old baby girl who had just been brought to the hospital ED by her parents. Now, while they were discussing her case, it was my turn to examine her—the generally superfluous medical student exam that doesn't contribute to care but is a learning exercise.

Pulling aside the curtains surrounding the infant's crib, I saw LaVonda lying disturbingly still. Her breathing seemed sluggish. I tapped her on her arm—she didn't respond. Her blank stare into space didn't change. I listened to her heart and her lungs, felt her neck, looked in her mouth. I didn't find anything abnormal.

Then I felt her belly. Something wasn't right—it was firmer than it should be, especially on her right side. Gradually I inched my hands down from her ribs. I was trying to find the edge of her liver. You usually can feel the liver's edge just below the rib cage. But the edge of this baby's liver was much lower than it should be—her liver filled most of her abdomen!

After leaving LaVonda, I found the resident. "Wow, that baby has a huge liver," I said. He looked at me, turned pale, and promptly went back to examine her again.

We were taught that the most important information a doctor can have is a patient's history: the symptoms, how they had progressed or changed, past episodes of disease. We were taught

that what a patient tells you is more important than tests—
blood tests, x-rays, or any type of test. If you had to choose
between talking to a patient or seeing test results, you should
choose talking. From this information, you create a differential
diagnosis—a list of disease or conditions to investigate through
testing so you can make a diagnosis.

In pediatrics, however, most patients haven't yet learned to
talk, so they can't give you a history. "Pediatrics is a lot like vet-
erinary medicine," one saying went.

So LaVonda couldn't give us a history. Maybe something
had happened, like she ingested something poisonous while
crawling around—she was just at that age when crawling begins,
and babies put all sorts of things in their mouths. But we didn't
know. She couldn't tell us.

We did know that she had had a cold and then became
lethargic. Her parents got worried and brought her to the
ER. Lethargy in an infant can indicate a very serious medical
problem. LaVonda was clearly very ill, so she was admitted to
the hospital's pediatric ICU and put on supportive treatment:
IV fluids and breathing support.

The doctors did a large number of tests to figure out what
was wrong with her. The resident consulted with the attending
physician. The attending physician called University Hospital
and discussed the case with pediatric faculty members, a
couple of whom came to see LaVonda.

None of them could make a diagnosis. In a last-ditch effort,
they gave her IV steroids. No one knew what else to do.

I thought this could be a SOAP note for the chart:
- Subjective—patient can't report anything.
- Objective—nonresponsive; enlarged liver.
- Assessment—we have no idea.
- Plan—supportive care; try steroids.

Two days after she came to the hospital, LaVonda was
dead. Someone said, "It was like God put his thumb down and
squashed her."

Looking back, I think LaVonda may have had Reye's syndrome. At the time, in the mid-1970s, the syndrome wasn't widely recognized. Reye's syndrome can follow a viral illness, like a cold or the flu. Symptoms include nausea, vomiting, and lethargy. The liver is often enlarged.

The syndrome is rare, but when it occurs, it's usually in very young children. It can be life-threatening and progress rapidly to death.

Epidemiology studies have found that Reye's syndrome is associated with aspirin use, so people today are told not to give aspirin to young children. But even today, the cause is not really clear, and all that is available is supportive care.

For some patients for some conditions, like for LaVonda, there is no treatment, there is no cure, and there may be no prevention. We know so little about so many things.

In A Coma Again

A lice, a 16-year-old with Type 1 diabetes, was lying on a gurney in the ED in 1978. Her blood glucose level was extremely high, and she was in a life-threatening coma.

The pancreas makes insulin, a hormone that enables glucose, a type of sugar, to move from the bloodstream into the cells of the body. That's how our body cells get the energy they need to function. But in Type 1 diabetes, the pancreas doesn't make insulin, and if there is no insulin, glucose can't enter the body's cells.

Type 1 diabetes is usually diagnosed early in life; it used to be called "juvenile diabetes."

[Type 2 diabetes, previously called "adult-onset diabetes," also results from problems with glucose in the blood not entering the cells, but the body does make some insulin, and so the condition is not as severe. Obesity is a risk factor for Type 2 diabetes; the condition is being seen more and more in youth because of the current obesity epidemic in developed countries.]

Cells need energy from somewhere, so if glucose can't get into the cells, the body breaks down fat for energy. The breakdown creates ketones, which are poisonous and can cause a life-threatening coma. That's what had happened to Alice. She was in a diabetic ketoacidotic coma. She was admitted to the ICU and given IV fluids and insulin.

Within a day or two, Alice had awakened from her coma.

After several days of treatment, she was stable and doing quite well—that's when I got a chance to talk with her. I asked Alice what had happened. She said that she "just didn't feel like" giving herself insulin shots.

In the 1970s, when I saw Alice, diabetic patients would test their urine for sugar using a dipstick—a small plastic stick with squares of filter paper that have been soaked with chemicals. The squares change color when there is sugar in the urine; there isn't supposed to be any. [Doctors used to taste urine to diagnose diabetes, before there were chemical tests. Yuck.]

At the time, there were a couple of types of insulin available that differed in how quickly they worked and how long it took for them to wear off. They were (and still are) injected into the skin using a tiny needle. Sometimes two or more insulins are given at the same time, for example, a shorter-acting and a longer-acting insulin.

Alice went to diabetes classes in the hospital. They taught her how, and how often, to check the sugar in her urine using a dipstick, how much of what type of insulin to give herself, how to use the needle to deliver the insulin, and when to give it depending on the dipstick results and when she was eating.

She passed the class and was discharged home from the hospital, armed with the knowledge of how to take care of her diabetes. The resident said they had "tuned her up."

Three weeks after she went home, Alice was back in the ED in another diabetic ketoacidotic coma. How could this have happened again—especially so soon?

Maybe it was a bigger issue than she "just didn't feel like" giving herself the insulin. Looking back on it, I wonder what else she needed to help her take care of herself. Did she need something in addition to medical treatment and instruction? Maybe the instruction wasn't clear enough. Maybe she had depression or a suicidal tendency. Maybe it was a call for help. I wonder if she ever got a psychiatric evaluation or behavioral counseling.

I don't remember those options being mentioned when we discussed her case during rounds. And I didn't know enough, and was too shy, to ask.

Today people with diabetes prick their fingers with small lancets and use a home glucose meter to test their blood sugar levels. It's a lot more accurate than a urine dipstick test. More kinds of insulin are available, as are insulin pumps, which mimic the body's provision of insulin over time.

We didn't know it then, but we know now based on results from clinical trials, that keeping blood sugar low not only keeps people with Type 1 diabetes out of ketoacidotic coma, but also reduces long-term complications of diabetes that occur in the eyes, nerves, and kidneys. But I wouldn't be surprised to hear that Alice didn't live long enough even to be a candidate for those long-term complications.

Several years later I was involved in a large randomized trial to determine whether treating people with Type 2 diabetes intensively—reducing their blood glucose so it was in the normal range—would reduce cardiovascular disease rates, which they often developed.

Spoiler Alert: it didn't.

DIAGNOSIS

I'm walking carefully down the sidewalk, passing by storefronts after picking up some things at the drug store. I bought a cane at the store because I'm uncoordinated and afraid of falling again. I've been waiting to find out the results of my medical tests.

My cell phone rings. I stop, hang the cane on my arm, and fish my phone out of my purse. It's Dr. Andrew, my primary care physician.

"I have good news, and not so good news," she says. "The brain MRI is normal—so you don't have a brain tumor."

I breathe a sigh of relief! I seriously had been worrying about having a brain tumor—worry that kept me awake at night.

"But your neck MRI shows some arthritic pathology and narrowing of the foramina." She knows I'm a physician, and so I know she means narrowing of the openings where nerves exit from the bony spinal column. "The nerves might be compressed, causing your arm symptoms." She tells me to follow up with the orthopedist and also gives me the name of neurosurgeon.

Neck arthritis is causing my arm symptoms!? This is good news. It sounds like something that could be fixed with neck surgery. I don't have a brain tumor!

I go to my orthopedist again for a follow-up on my frozen shoulder. My shoulder is better. He got the results of the nerve conduction test, and he tells me it was normal. "If arthritic changes in your neck

are interfering with the nerves down your arm," he says, "that test should not be normal. It should show reduced nerve conduction from your neck down your arm."

It isn't a neck problem, after all. Something else is going on.

He says, "I see you have a bit of a tremor," pointing to my left hand. I hadn't noticed that before. "You should go see a neurologist," he advises.

"I fell. Now I have a stiff arm and frozen shoulder. I'm really uncomfortable," I tell the neurologist. "My fingers are uncoordinated. My leg is awkward and shakes. My orthopedist noticed a tremor in my hand. All of this is just on my left side. I brought results of MRIs and a nerve conduction study."

The elderly neurologist has a sparse head of white hair. I think it must be 40 years since he was in training. I wonder if he keeps up. On the other hand, he must have seen a lot of patients over the years, and he has a great reputation with the orthopedist that referred me.

It must be the way I describe my symptoms, because Dr. Satinsky asks if I'm a physician. I admit that I am, but I don't see patients—I do research. I don't tell him that I haven't seen a patient in 25, no 30, years.

"Sit up here on the exam table," he says. I get on the table with some difficulty.

He holds his finger up about a foot and half away from my face. "Now touch your nose, then my finger, back and forth as fast as you can." First with one hand, then with the other—my left hand is much slower than my right, and it shakes.

"Open and close your right hand over and over," he says. While I'm opening and closing my right hand, he checks how easily he can move my other arm, my left arm. Then he checks the other side the same way. He tests my reflexes with his rubber hammer.

"Now hop down off the table and walk down the hall." He watches me walk. My left arm doesn't swing. "Turn around and walk back. Good. Now let's look at those test results."

I hand him a paper with results from the nerve conduction study, an x-ray film of an MRI of my lower back, and a computer disk with MRIs of my brain and neck.

He reads the nerve conduction results—normal. Then he leads me across the hall to his office and puts the disk into his computer. The MRIs come up on the screen. He looks at them closely, moving a cursor around to see different regions and zooming in on some areas.

He sees something in my neck that he's unsure of and phones a radiologist from the next office to come over and look at it with him. A couple of minutes later, the radiologist is there.

"I see something—there, in her neck. Is that something?" Dr. Satinsky asks the radiologist.

They zoom in on it. I marvel at the technology—I can see every bone and tissue. When I was in training, they couldn't look so clearly into someone's body through imaging.

"Hmmm...it looks.... no, it's not anything. It's nothing," says the radiologist.

The radiologist leaves, and Dr. Satinsky shows me the MRIs on the computer screen. "There's no tumor in your brain. Here's your neck...there are some changes, here, and here. But they're not bad, not bad at all."

I follow him back to the examining room, we sit down, and he summarizes: "There's no brain tumor, not enough pathology in your neck to cause your arm problems, no reduction of nerve conduction from your neck to your arm—basically I found no cause for your symptoms.

"But you have rigidity, a tremor, and uncoordination of your left hand. I also found ratcheting, or cogwheeling, of your left arm"—in other words, it didn't move smoothly when he moved it.

I vaguely remember something from medical school about these symptoms and findings. Now what was that condition?

Then he says, very matter-of-factly: "You have Parkinson's Disease."

Now I remember—that's what it was: Parkinson's Disease. I remember that Parkinson's Disease has no specific test. A diagnosis is made by excluding other causes and by the symptoms and physical exam.

    "It often starts on only one side of the body," Dr. Satinsky adds.

    After three months of symptoms, I'm actually relieved to have a diagnosis. And having Parkinson's is better than having a brain tumor or ALS. Parkinson's can be treated!

    Dr. Satinsky prescribes Sinemet, the mainstay drug for the condition. It will confirm the diagnosis if it reduces the symptoms. I'm so uncomfortable that I can't wait to take it. I get the prescription filled right away and take the first dose that evening. Within twenty minutes, my symptoms improve—reduced rigidity and tremor, improved coordination.

    Right there, the diagnosis is confirmed. I have Parkinson's Disease. My future is no longer a mystery.

PART 3: MAYBE I SHOULD QUIT

"Your life works to the degree you keep your agreements."

—*Werner Erhard*

A Bag Of Cement

Disco songs topped the charts, and I loved to dance. I had a dance partner, Ron, who taught me how to Lindy, and we learned to disco dance by watching the other dancers. But in 1978 I had little time to go dancing. I was in the middle of clinical rotations in my fourth year of medical school and on-call, staying overnight in the hospital, every third night.

My boyfriend Jerry, my roommate Sharon, and I were in our small two-bedroom apartment in the city, sitting around after dinner when Sharon asked us, "What's this?" Then she breathed hard and made a wheezing sound when she exhaled, pursing her lips.

Jerry said, "COPD." [Chronic Obstructive Pulmonary Disease]

"Right. How about this?" Sharon stood up and walked bent forward at the waist, not moving either arm, shuffling her feet, and then bumped into a wall.

Jerry said, "Parkinson's Disease."

I snuck off to my bedroom, got in bed, and pulled the covers up to my chin. I didn't think Sharon's imitations were mean. But I didn't think they were funny either.

Sharon and Jerry stayed in the other room, talking about the patients they had seen and what they had done that day during their clinical rotations. But I had no interest in talking about my day or the patients I had seen. I was trying to forget them.

When they were finished talking, Jerry crawled into bed with me and held me tight to comfort me.

Jerry often consoled me when I was depressed about school. Today, he is an accomplished emergency room physician. It's the perfect job for someone like him—smart and eager to solve whatever challenge comes through the door next.

Sharon was a former nurse who wanted to give orders to the doctors—she was tired of it being the other way around. She was smarter than most of the doctors, and I completely understood her motivations.

Sharon and Jerry both loved medicine. For me, it was a different story. The extensive memorization during the first two years of medical school was overwhelming and not interesting to me. Though I had skipped class a lot (after all we did have a note-taking service), I had done just fine on the tests.

But during the clinical years, we had to be there all the time. We were seeing patients who were very ill. Some we could help, but others were dying and there was nothing we could do for them. Not to mention the patients who stank, vomited on you, or were mean to you.

It was like dragging a bag of cement to get up in the morning. So, after three and a half years in medical school, I wondered whether medicine was the right career for me.

The Assistant Dean saw me soon after I made an appointment. I sat down in her dark office with mahogany wood paneling, her large desk between us.

A middle-aged woman with brown hair and a friendly face familiar to all us medical students, Dr. Sigman asked me, "What can I do for you?"

"I'm having a hard time," I told her. "I'm depressed. I don't like medical school, and I'm not sure being a doctor is for me."

She looked down at an open folder on her desk—apparently my grades and evaluations. Shuffling through some of the papers, she looked up at me and said, "But you're doing very well. You have good grades and good evaluations from your clinical rotations." She paused. "So don't think of quitting. We won't let you quit."

In medical school, if you get in, they do whatever it takes for you to finish and get that degree. I had heard that sometimes students are put on less-demanding schedules and given extra time to complete the education.

"We'll give you a leave of absence for a year," she said. "I want you to go see this psychologist." She handed me a business card. "You don't have to pay for the visits. He'll tell you how often to see him and let you know when you can stop. After the year is up, I want you to come back and finish medical school."

I wondered if this was a good idea. If I could just quit, I would put it all behind me. I had no idea what I would do next—but at least I'd be out of a situation I hated and depressed me. I looked at the business card and, wondering if this was right for me, said, "Okay."

That evening I found myself sitting on the floor of my bedroom, rocking back and forth holding my knees, with tears streaming down my face. I cried for Mr. Harris, who had come to the hospital to die. I cried for Mrs. Pigeon, who died on the operating table without seeing her daughter one last time. I cried for Alice, who kept relapsing into comas from her diabetes. I cried for LaVonda, the baby who had died for unknown reasons.

For an hour, I cried for them all.

PLATO Knows My Name

T he summer of 1978 was hot. I had just plunged into the swimming pool at my apartment building and was lying on the lounge chair at the pool's edge, trying to read a novel. But it wasn't holding my interest. My attention span was short; my mind kept wandering. My year's leave of absence from medical school had started, and it seemed I had a huge amount of time on my hands. What should do with my time—and with my life? At least I needed to make some money for living expenses while I figured it out.

What about computers? I thought. I had learned how to program a simple computer in college—one that ran the Skinner boxes where we studied pecking behaviors of pigeons. For another course, I would turn in a stack of punch cards to be run through a room-sized computer. In a few days, I would pick up the results, which usually were that there was a bug somewhere that I had to locate and fix.

It was clear that computers were the future. Computer programming was logical, and I needed something logical in my life. I decided to take an evening course to learn about computers.

I located the classroom in the darkened office building, after hours when most of the workers had gone home. There were about 20 people—almost all men—in the class. After introducing himself, the instructor asked each of us what we did, why we were there. Some had day jobs in construction or landscaping, some were out of work or finished with school, all were trying to better themselves, to get a job, or to move up to higher paying jobs.

The instructor taught the basics: what is a CPU, what is RAM, what is hardware, what is software. He seemed surprised when I got all the answers correct on an exam, but these basics were a piece of cake compared with the extensive memorization I had done in medical school. We hadn't gotten to anything difficult —at least not yet.

I wasn't sure where taking this course was leading, and I needed to make some money because there were no student loans for that year. Then it came to me: maybe I could get a job working on PLATO, the new teaching computer in the medical library.

"PLATO" stood for Programmed Logic for Automated Teaching Operations. I would log into the system, and the computer screen would read, "What is your name?" I would type my name, and the next time I logged in, PLATO would start with "Hello, Denise." I was fascinated. I even had a four-inch metal button pin that said, "PLATO Knows My Name."

During a month-long elective period in medical school, I had worked with one of the hematology professors to develop a short PLATO program that taught about hemoglobin—how the protein curves and coils around in a three-dimensional shape, which enables it to capture oxygen.

So I went to see the man in charge of PLATO in the medical school library. He referred me to Jim at Control Data Corporation (not to be confused with the other CDC, the Centers for Disease Control), which made and programmed the PLATO computers. The CDC office was in downtown Baltimore, just a 20-minute bus ride from my apartment.

The job interview went well, and so I got a job to design PLATO learning programs. My topics would be the sciences. I didn't tell them I was on a leave of absence for a year, because I didn't think I was going back to medical school.

The philosophy behind the PLATO educational programs was this: In regular teaching, the amount of time spent teaching is the same for all the students, but the amount students learn varies. In computer-assisted instruction, the amount of time spent varies, because the student can learn at his or her own pace, but the amount learned is the same. In other words, the computer courses were designed for students to keep at it for however long it might take them to learn the material—theoretically, it could range from a day to years. The assumption was that everybody could learn. The company was investing a lot of resources into computer-assisted instruction, banking on it becoming profitable—hoping it would be adopted broadly as a new way to teach.

They trained me to design teaching programs using a user-friendly programming interface, so I didn't have to learn a computer programming language. I was taught to have PLATO ask the student a question, and depending on the answer, to take the student to different feedback texts, personalized with the student's name embedded in the text, and down different paths. The programs would provide immediate positive reinforcement (like the B.F. Skinner studies), or correction if needed.

"Denise, where does food go after the stomach?" The screen would read.

"Duodenum," I would type.

"The duodenum, you said. That is correct, Denise."

Or I would type "colon," to test it.

"I'm sorry, colon is not the correct answer, Denise. Please hit NEXT to look at the drawing again." If it had spoken, it would have sounded like HAL in 2001 a Space Odyssey. But it wouldn't have passed the "Turing test," where someone couldn't tell whether it was a computer or a real person.

I learned to create pretests so students could skip material they already knew, and post-tests to determine whether they had learned everything they were supposed to. If they didn't, they were plunged right back into the program. The learning approach was based on Skinner's operant conditioning, in that the student received immediate feedback (reinforcement) throughout the computer-assisted instruction program.

It's unfortunate that today, some 40 years later, computerized training courses often don't use the technology in the flexible way it could be used. Instead, it's like reading a book on the screen. (Of course, we do that, too.) For the most recent training course I took at work, which was about human subjects research, I didn't read any of it—I just hit 'enter' over and over, screen after screen of information that required no interaction, until I got to the end and took the test. I passed with only one wrong answer. What a waste of time; they should have had a pretest.

PLATO ran on a closed network designed just for PLATO—dumb computer terminals connected to a mainframe. This was before the Internet had come of age, but PLATO was innovative, with features that were ahead of its time: It had personal messages (like email), real-time chatting across the bottom of the screen (like instant messaging), and chat rooms (similar to Facebook but each chat room had a specific topic). It even had a touch screen. Though innovative and with a lot of potential, PLATO failed in comparison to the upcoming Internet and Web, which would take over.

I had been working on PLATO for almost a year, and my medical school leave of absence was almost up. Seeing the psychologist during that year helped me think about whether

I wanted to finish medical school. He had me thinking about alternatives. For example, he had me take a test about my interests, which came up that I should be a librarian. But I didn't think that would be the best occupation for me. Maybe I should be a lab scientist. Or continue working on computers.

At least my time away from sick and dying patients had helped me recover from my depression. But I was at sea, struggling with what to do next. I still hadn't decided whether to go back to medical school. I needed to do something that would help me decide.

Nothing To Get

"**Y**ou should go," said Robert, my tall, dark, handsome, Jewish ex-husband with whom I had been married for two years during college because we wanted to live together (but people didn't just live together back in the 1970s). I was still good friends with him despite a rough patch where we decided to get divorced. He followed in my footsteps and went to medical school after he came with me to visit one of my classes. "There's a seminar coming up in a month," he added.

"Don't drink any coffee or tea in the morning," Ron told me. A classmate of mine that I used to date and was best friends with now, with whom I went disco dancing, Ron had recently taken the training. "It may be hours before you can go to the bathroom."

So Robert and Ron, two people I liked and respected, both recommended the Erhard Seminar Training (est). It wasn't cheap, but I was making a salary at Control Data Corporation. I thought it was probably just a bunch of hooey, but all I had to lose was two weekends of my time and about $300. So I signed up.

Early on a Saturday morning, I walked into the large hotel ballroom where they had set up rows and rows of folding chairs, about 500 chairs I guessed. Two aisles ran between the chairs, each aisle with a microphone on a stand. "Runners" stood at the back with cordless microphones, ready to pass them around for the attendees to speak.

I found a seat about two-thirds of the way back, a bit off to the side. I looked at the handout they had given me, which had audience rules for the seminar.

> • *No wearing watches.* I took off my watch and put it in my
> pocket.
> • *No eating.* I put my granola bar in my purse.
> • *No talking unless you are called upon.* That wouldn't be hard.
> I didn't plan on saying anything.
> • *No "voting" by clapping more for one person than for another
> —only clap five times.* Hmm… that's interesting.
> • *No taking bathroom breaks without the trainer saying there's
> a break.* Luckily I had heard about this last one and hadn't
> drunk much liquid with my breakfast.

I looked around. The audience was filling the seats. They were all ages, both sexes, mostly white. Some dressed nicely, some just wore jeans and a t-shirt.

After everyone was seated, a thin middle-aged white man climbed up the few stairs at the side of the stage, walked to the middle of the stage, and faced the audience. Our trainer. He stood silently—no podium, just him alone in the center of the stage with a microphone in his hand.

He scanned the audience as he paced slowly from one side of the stage to the other. The talking subsided. I could hear feet shuffling, small coughs, people settling in.

He stopped and faced the audience. "You're all assholes," he announced.

Nobody spoke. Nobody coughed. Nobody moved.

He scanned the audience again. "You're assholes because you don't know what you're doing in your life. You're assholes because you can't let go of things from your past. You're assholes because you can't communicate well."

He started pacing again, back and forth on the stage. "Remember when you were a teenager, and your mother wanted you to stay home for an evening?" he asked us. "All she wanted was for you to be there. That's all she wanted. But you went out anyway. You went out anyway! Was she really asking too much?"

I felt guilty, though I don't remember my mother ever asking me to stay home for an evening.

A young man raised his hand. The trainer called on him, and he stood up. The runner brought him a microphone. "But my mother was asking too much. It was painful to stay home … because she beat me." He was crying.

"I see you're holding onto this. You don't have to! It happened in the past. You could let it go and move into the future. It's your choice!" the trainer said. "Thank you for sharing." We all clapped five times. The young man sat back down.

"Now I want you all to close your eyes and just let yourself be. Think about your toes. Find a spot in your toes. Now relax your toes."

I closed my eyes and found my toes. I relaxed my toes.

"Now find a spot in your leg. Relax your leg."

I found a spot in my leg. I relaxed my leg.

Then we found spots in our butts, our waists, our backs, arms, necks, faces. We progressively relaxed our entire bodies. The woman next to me started crying. I had no idea why.

After about 15 minutes, the trainer told us to open our eyes. The room now seemed crystal clear—sharper than it had been when I had walked in. I was there—in the "now."

"Imagine that yesterday I gave you a choice between vanilla or chocolate ice cream," the trainer said. "You had vanilla. Looking back on it, you could have had chocolate, right?"

We all nodded our heads.

"No. That's not right. You had vanilla."

A middle-aged woman raised her hand, was called on, stood up, and said, "But I could have had chocolate."

"No. You had vanilla."

"I don't understand. I could have had chocolate."

"No," he said. "You had vanilla."

I got it. The past was the past. You couldn't have had choc-olate, because you didn't have chocolate. You can't change the past. And you can't change other people. But you can let go of things. Just let the past be and move toward the future.

Throughout the day, the trainer described different life situ-ations. People in the audience raised their hands and shared, asked questions, or disagreed.

At one point I raised my hand, stood up, and tried to explain something. I can't remember what it was, but I do remember I couldn't articulate what I wanted to say. I tried saying it several times, and he still didn't seem to understand. I gave up and sat down.

Was this a microcosm of my life? Giving up when things got too hard…maybe like medical school?

We left the seminar on Sunday evening with an assignment for the week—when we see other people, imagine that they are scared of us or intimidated by us.

I drove home, and everything I saw—the car, the stars in the sky, the lights on the road—had never appeared so clear. And for a week, everybody, even strangers I passed on the sidewalk, was intimidated by me.

And that week, I trained my cat! Every day when I'd come home from work, Taffy would run outside immediately when I opened the door. After just a couple of minutes, she would meow to be let back in, usually while I was in the middle of changing my clothes or fixing something to eat. It was annoy-ing.

But now I knew how to train her. I didn't say, as I usually did, "No, stop, don't go out," while opening the door only a crack and putting my foot in the way of her exit. Instead, I said, "Taffy, I want you to go outside now, but just for a little while. Meow when you want to come back in."

And she did! She went out. I waited a few minutes and then she came right back—just as I had told her to—meowing for me to let her in. I never knew how easy it was to train a cat.

The next weekend, I walked into the seminar room, this time looking forward to it. We had a different trainer—a blonde woman, dressed in a skirted suit with heels. There were two blank flipcharts of paper on the stage.

"Here is what you perceive," she said, pointing to one of the flipcharts.

She walked to the other side of the stage and pointed to the other flipchart. "And here is what is real. They are not the same."

Well, that's what I learned in psychology class—that our perceptions could distort reality.

She asked the audience what she should write on the "real" flipchart. People volunteered: the building, the chair they were sitting in, the floor, the drapes. She wrote each item on the chart.

Then she walked to the other side of the stage and asked what she should write on the "perceived" flipchart. People volunteered: happiness, love, anger, disappointment. She wrote those down.

Then we did another progressive relaxation exercise. I opened my eyes, and the room was bright and clear.

"Look hard at these charts," she commanded. "They are actually reversed. Over here are things we think are real...but they are actually what we perceive." Walking to the other side of the stage, "And over here, things we perceive... well, these things are actually real."

Whoa.

"Perceptions are powerful," she continued. "And you have control over your perceptions! You can refuse to accept what happened in the past, or you can accept it—just let it be—but you cannot change the past. Whether you accept it...well, that's your choice. It's up to you."

There was murmuring throughout the room.

"You have heard, I am sure, that by the end of this training you would 'get it.'" She paused and looked slowly from one side of the audience to the other. "Well, what is it?" she asked. "What do you think you should get?"

Audience members raised their hands, stood up, and said what they thought they should get: You can't change the past. You should love one another. You should be in the present. You should help other people. You should accept yourself as you are.

After each one, the trainer said, "Thank you for sharing," and we all clapped five times.

"What your mates here are telling us, is that we give our own lives meaning," she concluded. "That's right. There is nothing more to get."

I got it. And I believed it—there is no meaning to life than the meaning we give it.

But I needed my life to mean something. Otherwise, why was I here on Earth? Could helping people be the meaning I give to my life? Isn't that why I started medical school in the first place?

Should I go back to medical school?

If I went back, I needed to commit to finishing. I couldn't quit like I wanted to when I went to see the Associate Dean. I couldn't quit like I did the first weekend of the est training, when I couldn't explain what I was trying to say to the trainer and gave up.

Even if I didn't do clinical medicine, a medical degree would be a doorway to a job where I could make a difference—where I could work to help people. And now that I knew what to expect seeing patients, I thought I could handle it.

So I decided to finish medical school. To give meaning to my life. To move forward. To make a difference.

SECOND OPINION

*B*ruce (my husband) and I decide to get a second opinion, so we drive about an hour to Baltimore at 8:30 in the morning, a week after Dr. Satinsky diagnosed Parkinson's Disease in 2011. He had started me on medication, which helped, but we wanted to see an expert in movement disorders.

I had made an appointment with Dr. Weiner, the head of neurology at the University of Maryland School of Medicine, my alma mater, and director of the movement disorders center. He had published clinical guidance about Parkinson's based on systematic evidence reviews—a method I use in my work and believe in. I found him after an Internet search and thought he was the perfect doctor to see. A patient had canceled, so when I called, I got an appointment for the next morning,

When Michael J. Fox testified in Congress about the need for stem cell research, his Parkinson's symptoms were prominent. He was accused of stopping his medications for effect. I remember that and stop taking my medication after I make the appointment, so the doctor can see my unmedicated symptoms.

◆ ◆ ◆

"Here's a written test to fill out," says the receptionist, handing me some papers. Sitting in the waiting room with Bruce, I take the test:
• Do you have a tremor? (Yes)

- *Can you stand up without pushing on chair arms? (Yes)*
- *Do you have difficulty swallowing? (No)*
- *Do you have difficulty buttoning your shirt? (Not often)*
- *Do you have difficulty with speech? (No)*
- *Is your handwriting normal? (Yes)*
- *Do you walk normally? (No, my left arm doesn't swing)*
- *Do you freeze when walking? (No)*
- *Have you fallen? (Yes)*
- *Can you roll over in bed by yourself? (Yes)*
- *Are you bedridden? (No)*

"Bruce, do you see what kinds of questions they ask? About being bedridden and unable to turn over in bed. We need to prepare for these things." I'm thinking about my Dad's ALS; we were never prepared for his rapid disease progression.

A nurse calls my name. "Come on to the back," she says. "I have some cognitive tests for you to take." We get up and follow her down the hall toward the examination rooms.

"Here's a chair for you." She points to a chair across from a small desk. I sit down while Bruce stands by my chair. She sits across from me at the desk.

"First, I want you to start with the number 100 and subtract 7 over and over again—you can't write it down." I know about this test, but I had never tried it myself. I close my eye to visualize the subtractions and say, "100, 93...86... 79, 72... 65." It's hard. She writes the numbers down as I say them.

"That's enough, you can stop." Then she pulls out a stopwatch. "Now, how many words can you think of that start with the letter F?"

I pause a moment; at first, no words come to mind. Then I say, "finger, father, feather, frost ....further....far....fork...forward... fancy." She writes down each word— "Stop," and clicks the stopwatch. Later I wonder how I could not have thought of the most obvious F word!

She tells me that my score is average. I don't necessarily think this is good news. Isn't my cognitive ability usually above average?

Next, a nurse escorts us to an exam room, where a neurology

fellow thoroughly questions me. The fellow would have already gone to medical school, done an internship and two more years of an internal medicine residency, and then the neurology fellowship he's in now. He asks more questions than Dr. Satinsky had asked. I describe all my symptoms, and I give him the test results.

The fellow examines me, doing similar tests as Dr. Satinsky had done, but adding foot slapping—how fast can I slap the front of my foot on the floor, not lifting my heels. First my right foot (slap, slap, slap, slap), then my left foot (slap…slap…slap). My left foot is noticeably slower. He asks me to stand up and pulls me from behind by my shoulders to see how well I can keep my balance. I lose balance but recover without him having to catch me.

A medical student is with us in the examining room, taking it all in. He looks a bit confused or uncomfortable. He reminds me of myself as a third-year medical student doing my first clinical rotation.

The fellow and student leave, presumably to talk to Dr. Weiner. After a few minutes, Dr. Weiner comes into the exam room along with the fellow and student. He asks me a couple of questions and briefly examines me. Then he says, "You have Parkinsonism." I wonder if that means I have Parkinson's Disease. Maybe he's just trying to break the news gently because "Parkinsonism" can be a side effect of some medications, but I'm not on any medications except for the Sinemet I had just started. So he has confirmed the diagnosis.

The fellow tells us that the rigidity from the Parkinson's prevented the natural movement of my arm, so that's why I couldn't swing my arm and got a frozen shoulder. He says this is a fairly common presenting symptom for Parkinson's.

Standing to leave, I ask the medical student, "Did you learn something today?" He says yes, he did. I say, "good." But he looks worried. Is he worried about me? I hope he cares about his patients, but I also hope he doesn't go home and cry when a patient dies, like I did.

Two neurologists have now diagnosed me as having Parkinson's. Over a couple of months, I have seen my primary care doctor twice, three orthopedists, two neurologists, a neurosurgeon, and two physiatrists. I'm lucky to get a diagnosis this quickly; for some people it takes years.

I go back to my primary care doctor, Dr. Andrew, and tell her about the diagnosis. Her eyes tear up. She hugs me and asks how I'm doing. (Depressed, devastated, shocked.) "I'm doing okay," I say. She is the only doctor who has shown empathy. Perhaps that's because she is the only woman doctor of all the doctors I saw.

In my medical training, I had learned about Parkinson's disease—but from a doctor's point of view, not a patient's point of view. I had learned that Parkinson's patients don't swing their arms; I didn't know their arms felt stiff and hurt, as mine did. I had learned that Parkinson's patients have a tremor; I didn't realize they are uncoordinated, drop things, and have problems typing and writing, as I was having. I had learned that Parkinson's patients have difficulty starting and stopping when they walk; I didn't know those problems come later; that at first, symptoms are only on one side of the body, like mine were.

I needed to learn more about the condition. So I started reading about it. I found the "Hoehn And Yahr Staging Scale," which is used to stage the disease. I learned that, though medication can help control symptoms, it doesn't stop progression down the stages.

Below are the stages of Parkinson's disease based on the Modified Hoehn And Yahr Staging Scale (parentheses added by me). I'm at Stage 1 or maybe 1.5.

- *STAGE 0 = No signs of disease*
- *STAGE 1 = Unilateral disease (one side of the body)*
- *STAGE 1.5 = Unilateral plus axial involvement (one side of the body plus trunk involvement, like poor posture)*
- *STAGE 2 = Bilateral disease (both sides of the body), without impairment of balance*
- *STAGE 2.5 = Mild bilateral disease, with recovery on pull test (the examiner stands behind the patient and then pulls the patient back briskly to see if the patient can recover his/her balance)*
- *STAGE 3 = Mild to moderate bilateral disease; some postural*

(standing) instability; physically independent.

• STAGE 4 = Severe disability; still able to walk or stand unassisted

• STAGE 5 = Wheelchair-bound or bedridden unless aided

The Unified Parkinson's Disease Rating Scale (UPDRS) is another rating system, which is used to follow disease progression.

I locate the test on the Internet and score myself—18 out of 199. A score of zero is no Parkinson's.

I have low scores on both scales, so it isn't bad—but it will, I expect, get a lot worse.

PART 4: A POPULATION PERSPECTIVE

"Medicine is a social science, and politics is nothing else but medicine on a large scale."

—Rudolf Virchow, 1848

Truth About Medicine

Ten of us doing a radiology rotation in 1979 were there when Dr. Rocky—a big burly man with a dark beard—closed the door to the classroom. I had chosen radiology for my first rotation after returning to medical school because it was easy—no night call, no patients of your own.

"Don't tell anybody about this—but it's about time you knew the truth about medicine," he said.

The truth? What was he talking about? Weren't we here to learn about radiology? But Dr. Rocky had no x-rays to show us. He just had a blackboard and a piece of chalk, and ten fourth-year medical students looking at him.

Drawing a horizontal line across the bottom of the chalkboard from left to right, Dr. Rocky said, "This line shows the timeline from the early 1700s to today—the late 1970s."

Then he drew a vertical line going up from the left of the horizontal line. "This line is the mortality rate," he said. He was drawing the axes of a graph.

Starting at the top left, he drew a line that went gradually down to the right, approaching zero as it reached the right-hand edge of the blackboard. "This is the U.K.'s annual mortality rate from tuberculosis. It was very high in the 1700s, and it's very low today—almost zero."

He turned to face the class. "Why do you think the mortality rate decreased so much?"

Two students raised their hands. Dr. Rocky called on one.

"Antibiotics," the student said.

"Well, here's where they started to use antibiotics for TB." He drew an arrow on the graph about three-quarters of the way toward the right—after the line had declined a lot. "What happened before antibiotics?" He waited. Nobody volunteered an answer.

Then Dr. Rocky drew a circle at about the middle of the graph. "Here's when germ theory was being developed. And here [putting an X] is where they identified the tubercle bacillus," which is the germ that causes TB.

The death rate had declined a lot before anybody even knew germs existed, before they identified the TB germ, and well before antibiotics were available to treat the disease.

"So what happened earlier?" he asked. "Why did the mortality rate decline so much?"

I had no idea what happened earlier. The ice age?

"Well, I'll tell you. There was better agriculture, refrigeration, and better nutrition. Cities started cleaning up garbage and developing sanitation systems to clean water. People stopped throwing waste out of their windows. Living conditions improved."

He looked around the room. I don't know whether this information impressed the others, but it impressed me. Seeing patients is important, of course—we treat their illnesses, we improve their lives. But the environment also affects health— in a broader way for more people at a time. And that's how I was introduced to public health—by a radiologist, of all people!

What Should We Eat?

The Krebs cycle (also called the citric acid cycle) is a vital part of nutritional science. This biochemical cycle is part of a complex sequence of events that converts macronutrients (nutrients that have calories: carbohydrates, fats, and proteins) into energy for the body to function. Enzymes react with molecules in a chain of reactions that cycles back to the first molecule. The process uses oxygen, creates carbon dioxide, and produces energy to be used by the cells.

In my first year of medical school, we had learned about the Krebs cycle and were tested on it. But I wasn't taught anything about what people should actually eat until my fourth year of medical school, when a tall thin man with a trim beard and a British accent gave us a lecture on adult ambulatory care (outpatient care).

"The American Heart Association prudent diet," Dr. Sherwin told the class, "is designed to help reduce heart disease—the leading cause of death in the United States." This was the first time I remember hearing what the leading cause of death was.

"There are different types of fats in food," he continued. "We know from research that saturated fat raises low-density-lipoprotein cholesterol—LDL cholesterol—in the blood. We also know that elevated LDL cholesterol is associated with higher rates of heart disease. So the AHA concluded that people should eat less saturated fat. Cholesterol in the diet matters less than saturated fats do."

So basically, it wasn't the cholesterol that you ate that mattered for blood cholesterol, it was the type of fat? I didn't know that.

"Saturated fat comes from animal sources—like meat and cheese," he said. "Polyunsaturated fats are better for you—they come from vegetable sources, like corn or safflower.

"The AHA recommends eating complex carbohydrates like starches in bread, not simple carbohydrates, which are sugars, like in candies and sodas. They say to eat less fatty meats and cheese, and to use vegetable oils, which have polyunsaturated fats, instead of animal fat, which is mostly saturated fat."

That lecture by Dr. Sherwin near the end of my fourth, and last, year of medical school—was my first real exposure to health behaviors to prevent disease. Why didn't they teach us about diet earlier? What about other approaches to prevention? Were they keeping them a secret?

The cynic in me thinks that medical training perhaps has been based on the assumption—maybe unrecognized, clearly unstated—that medicine is a business. If prevention were successful, fewer people would seek healthcare services, which the healthcare industry and physicians provide to make money. Is that why medical schools don't teach much, and doctors don't do much, about prevention? Is prevention, perhaps, inconsistent with the business model?

By then, the fourth year in medical school, almost all of my classmates had decided what kind of doctor they would be: a generalist who goes into family practice, internal medicine, or pediatrics, or a specialist who goes into ophthalmology, cardiology, urology, oncology, or neurology, etc. (a lot of "-ologies"). As one saying goes: "A specialist is someone who learns more and more about less and less, until he knows everything about nothing. A generalist is someone who learns less and less about more and more, until he knows nothing about everything." And I would add: "Whether generalist or specialist, most physicians don't know much about nutrition or diet!"

Unlike the other fourth-year medical students in Dr. Sherwin's lecture, I was still trying to figure out what to do after medical school. Now that I had been exposed to public health, I wanted to explore that as a specialty.

I found out that there is board certification in the field of *preventive medicine and public health*, just like there is board certification in other medical specialties. Generally, you are eligible to take a board exam after three years of training past medical school. (Always look for board certification when you choose a doctor!) I discovered that there was a preventive medicine residency at the medical school in Dr. Sherwin's department. I also was interested in family medicine, because I thought that was the specialty where prevention could best be incorporated into practice.

So, my graduation from medical school on the horizon, I went to see the directors of the residencies for both family medicine and preventive medicine. For some time, they had wanted to create a combined residency in family medicine and preventive medicine, and they asked me if I would be the guinea pig. I said, of course! It was just what I wanted.

One way to combine training in two fields is to alternate half a year in each. So that's what we decided to do. I would be an intern in family medicine for six months—doing rotations in medical fields needed to take care of entire families: internal medicine, pediatrics, obstetrics-gynecology, dermatology, surgery. The next six months I would go to public health school. Then six months back in family practice, and a final six months back in public health school to complete a Master's in Public Health (MPH) degree. Board eligibility in preventive medicine requires an MPH (or equivalent) because so much of prevention is through population and environmental approaches (as I had learned from a radiologist, of all people!).

Based on personal experience, I think most physicians don't even know the field of preventive medicine exists. There are many specialists in the field, but they usually don't open medical practices. Instead, they become health department directors responsible for improving the health of communities, work for the government in policy or research, or work in academia in research and teaching.

So in 1980—when Jimmy Carter was president, Ordinary People won Best Picture, and John Lennon lived his last year (and I was 29), I finally started training in the field that would become my career: preventive medicine and public health.

Epidemiology

"Welcome to Introduction to Epidemiology," Dr. Gordis announced from the front of the large classroom at the Johns Hopkins School of Public Health. It was the beginning of the Fall 1980 term in the Master's of Public Health program. "What is epidemiology, you may be wondering. Here's one definition."

He projected a slide that read, Epidemiology: the study of the distribution and determinants of disease in human populations. "Other definitions add a statement about applying the findings to improve health in populations," he added.

Epidemiology is considered the basic science of public health—its methods underlie everything we do in the field—so this was a required course for an MPH degree. The term "epidemiology' comes from 'epidemic' (not from epidermis, which is skin). The methods originated with the study of epidemics.

Dr. Gordis described some history of epidemiology, including the story of the cholera epidemic in London in the 1800s. An English physician, John Snow (no, not the character in Game of Thrones), found that cholera cases clustered in an area supplied by one of the city's water sources. The government stopped delivering water from that source, and the cholera epidemic abated. Another example is the one I had heard from Dr. Rocky (a radiologist, of all people) that better nutrition and a cleaner environment over time led to lower TB death rates in the U.K.

In these examples, they didn't even know about germs! But they still improved public health by looking for exposures associated with higher risk of disease—and doing something about them. The lesson here is that even if we don't know the biological mechanisms by which an exposure to something causes a disease (the enzymes, reactions, germs, or genes), we still may be able to do something to reduce risk.

"There are two major approaches in the science of epidemiology," Dr. Gordis told us. "Descriptive epidemiology examines patterns of disease by person, place, and time, which helps us decide where to target public-health efforts. Analytic or etiologic epidemiology identifies exposures that may increase the risk of getting a disease, which possibly could be changed to prevent disease. We call these things risk factors. Identifying risk factors is the key point of the three major study designs in analytic epidemiology."

I used these study designs throughout my career, and I'll refer to them later, so I summarize them here:

- A *case-control study,* sometimes called a case-comparison study, compares people who have a disease with people who don't have the disease to see if past exposures differ.
- A *cohort study* compares people who are exposed to something (such as a personal health behavior, or something in the environment) with people not exposed to see if their future disease risks differ.
- A *randomized trial* (or randomized controlled trial—RCT) compares people who get an intervention (an exposure to something, a treatment, a diet, etc.) with people who don't get the intervention to see if the intervention results in differences in their future health status.

Epidemiology, as well as every other class I took in public health school—international health, maternal and child health, statistics, public health and the law, health education, healthcare administration—came from a population perspective. Going to public-health school opened my eyes to a bigger viewpoint.

And I learned a huge amount. Here are some examples of what I learned:

The leading causes of death and disabilities in the U.S. are chronic diseases such as heart disease and cancer. In 1900, the leading causes were infectious diseases such as influenza and tuberculosis. The change paralleled the industrial revolution, concomitant changes in lifestyle and diet, and the development of effective immunizations to control infectious diseases.

The major contributor to average life expectancy at birth is infant mortality; for example, the average life expectancy in China increased from 43 years in 1960 to 75 years in 2012, because infant mortality rates went down (not because people used to die at age 43).

People at lower socioeconomic levels (based on income and/or education) have higher mortality rates, higher disease rates, higher rates of smoking, more obesity, and poorer diets than people at higher socioeconomic levels; these disparities in health and risk factors are influenced by living conditions, which are ultimately affected by policies.

In nearly every class, students worked in small groups on problems or projects. One afternoon, sitting together in the student lounge waiting for the Friday happy hour to start, six of us were discussing our latest small group exercises. There was Mary Ann, a tall thin nurse who had trekked to villages in Nepal giving vaccinations to children, wearing her Birkenstock sandals as she walked for miles and miles. There was Judith, a visiting nurse in the U.S. who checked on patients in their homes, making sure they were all right and taking their medications; a single mother with a young daughter, Judith later became my roommate. There was Sam, a tall, dark-haired physician doing a preventive medicine residency who had a good sense of humor and was handsome like Burt Reynolds; we went on one date—to a Halloween party. There was Toby, also a physician, who seemed wide-eyed and a bit weird, but in a good way.

"The one about folks who got sick after a picnic was interesting. Finding out what people ate who got sick and comparing it to what people ate who didn't get sick."

"That's like what the Epidemiology Intelligence Service at CDC does when they investigate epidemics."

"Did you all figure out it was the potato salad?"

"No, we got the coleslaw." Ha, ha. "Oh, I'm just kidding."

"The problem with smokestacks and pollution was stupid—calculating how tall a smokestack should be so smoke will miss the local village. Sounds industrial, not like public health."

"Well, you know what they say, 'the solution to pollution is dilution.'"

"Did you hear we can get a copy of last year's epidemiology exams?"

"We should get together and go over them, to prepare for the upcoming test."

Every Friday, I met my MPH friends at happy hour, where faculty and students mingled over beer or wine in the student lounge. After a couple of drinks, we would go out to dinner. One Friday, it was my turn to organize going to dinner. Beer bottle in hand, walking through the lounge, I scouted for a man because we had too many women and needed balance.

Bruce, a health education professor on sabbatical from his university who was in my epidemiology and health services classes, was sitting in a chair against the wall chatting with someone I didn't know. I stopped and asked Bruce if he wanted to join us for dinner. He said he would. Then I had to go back and get him...twice, because he was so engrossed in his conversation.

ce and I sat next to each other at dinner. He was funny; I laughed a lot at his quips. At the end of dinner, he asked me if I could drive him home. He didn't have a car; you don't really need one in the middle of the city. In front of his apartment building, Bruce hesitated before getting out of my white 1973 VW beetle. He turned to me, looked me in the eyes, and asked, "Can I see you again?"

I was interested. He was fun and attractive, with a stylish white-person's Afro and hippie mustache. So I said, "sure."

"Hmmm…" he said. "Well…I'm not free until…" He paused. "…tomorrow." Cute.

The next day we had a great time visiting the zoo. Several months later, we got married. He told me that was the first and last time he had ever used that line. I almost believe him.

In addition to sweeping me off my feet, Bruce taught me a lot about health education and health promotion (his area of specialty)—especially that the purpose of health education is not just to convey knowledge, it's to help people engage in healthful behaviors.

We've been equal partners for nearly 40 years, though I still have to keep going back to get him when I'm ready to leave a party, and he's socializing.

Her Pressure Is Fine

After half a year pursuing an MPH degree, I returned to clinical medicine in 1981 to finish my family practice internship because I was alternating every six months between preventive medicine/public health and family practice. I continued to do rotations in specialties relevant to family practice—internal medicine, pediatrics, surgery. But now I had more responsibility.

My patient, Ms. Jones, sat across from me in the family practice clinic, where I saw patients a half day a week as part of my family practice residency. A 45-year-old African-American grandmother, she had brought her cute granddaughter with her.

"Let's check your blood pressure," I said. I asked her to remove her jacket, took the blood pressure cuff off the wall, wrapped it around her upper arm, placed my stethoscope bell inside her elbow, blew up the cuff, let the air out, and listened to the heart beats appear (systolic pressure), then disappear (diastolic pressure).

"Your diastolic pressure is 100," I told her. "That's a bit high."

Diastolic pressure, the second number in a blood pressure reading, indicates the pressure in your arteries when your heart relaxes. At the time, levels over 90 were considered elevated.

"Has a doctor ever told you that you have high blood pressure?" I asked.

She said, "No, not as far as I know."

"Let me take it again."

I retook her blood pressure after a few minutes, because sometimes just walking into a doctor's office can raise someone's blood pressure. It was still elevated.

I looked in her medical chart. Every time she had come in for the past three years, her blood pressure had been over 90 —diastolic pressures of 95, 100, 105, 110. She wasn't on any medications.

Just a few weeks earlier, at a journal club in the preventive medicine department, we had discussed a recent paper from the Hypertension Detection and Follow-up Program (HDFP), a randomized trial funded by the National Institutes of Health. The purpose of the study was to determine whether reducing BP in adults with diastolic pressures above 90 would reduce cardiovascular diseases compared to usual care, where treatment of BP down to that level wasn't the general practice at the time.

About 11,000 adults were randomly assigned to have their pressure reduced to below 90 by medications prescribed by study clinicians or to continue going to their own doctors to receive usual care. The group treated to the lower BP level had significantly lower rates of death and strokes over five years compared with the usual care group. This improvement in health outcomes had occurred even in patients with "mild hypertension" at the start of the study, defined as diastolic blood pressure between 90 and 105.

The study was of high quality. The prestigious NIH had funded it. The findings were convincing. And Ms. Jones, who was sitting right across from me in the clinic, was just like the patients in the study.

"Your blood pressure is a bit high. I think you have mild hypertension," I said and noted it on her medical chart. "I'm prescribing a diuretic. It will remove fluid through your kidneys. You may have to urinate more often than usual."

A diuretic was the first drug used in the HDFP in their "stepped care" treatment regimen, which called for adding hypertension drugs that worked by different mechanisms, one by one, until you lowered diastolic blood pressure to below 90.

I scheduled a follow-up visit to check how Mrs. Jones was doing on the medication. Unfortunately, the day of her visit I couldn't be there for some reason, so one of the attending physicians kindly saw my patients.

Reviewing the charts upon my return, I saw he had taken Ms. Jones off the diuretic.

"Thanks for seeing my patients," I said. "But why did you take Ms. Jones off the diuretic?"

"I took her blood pressure. It was fine. She doesn't need the medicine." I thought maybe her BP was fine because she was taking medicine for it. But I asked, "What about the HDFP results? They found that lowering diastolic pressure to below 90 reduced mortality and strokes."

"That's just one study," he said. "She doesn't need the medication."

Why doesn't he think the HDFP results are relevant for practice? I wondered. But I didn't say anything; I was too shy to ask, and certainly didn't want to argue with an attending physician.

It occurred to me later that maybe he didn't even know about the study, since it had just been published.

In my training in the 1970s, they taught us that blood pressure naturally goes up as people age, so a rise in blood pressure was okay.

Today, in 2019, this seems ridiculous. We have learned it's important, even for people with "mild" hypertension, to lower their elevated blood pressure regardless of their age, because doing so can reduce the risk of strokes, heart attacks, and death.

Later in my career when I worked on translating research findings into practice, I told Ms. Jones' story to my colleagues. When I got to the part where the attending physician told me that he took her blood pressure and it was fine, they laughed (even though it wasn't really funny).

Pregnant

My breasts were swollen; my period was late. I was in the middle of my family practice residency, on call in the hospital every third night, and now doing, of all things, an OB-GYN rotation. I was nauseated and throwing up every morning, getting four hours of sleep if I was lucky, but not showing yet. So nobody knew a pregnant woman was learning how to deliver other pregnant women's babies.

One evening I was sitting in the on-call room when my supervising resident in OB-GYN walked in. "A fat cow just came in," he said. "Regular contractions every five minutes. Her fourth baby. Let's go see her."

He walked out of the room. I followed, glaring at the back of his head. Though appalled by his language, I held my tongue.

The patient was lying on the examining table, her feet in the stirrups, a sheet draped over her legs. "You check her and then I'll check you," he said. "Ha-ha. That came out wrong, didn't it?" I cringed.

When it was my turn to examine her, I asked the patient how she was doing. I sat down on the stool between her open legs. The odor was foul. I tried to hold my nausea in check. "I'm going to put my hand inside you to check on the baby's progress, okay?" I put gloves on, slid my fingers into her vagina, and palpated to feel how far the uterus opening had dilated. We used numbers from one to ten to describe the degree of dilation. A ten meant the cervix was completely open, and the baby was ready to be pushed out.

"Well, counselor, what do you think?" he asked.

"She's about a five. I can feel the baby's head; it's not breach."

"Good," he said. "This is her fourth, so it'll probably go fast. Let's check her in 15."

We left the room. "Why can't these women stop?" he asked. "Dropping one after another. No wonder these people stay poor."

'These people'? I cringed again but tried to ignore him.

We checked the patient several times over about three hours. When she dilated to a ten, he told me, "You catch this one."

I sat again on the stool between the patient's legs. The baby's head was crowning. I held my hands near the mother's vaginal opening, ready to help ease the baby out. The nurse shouting "push, push" with each contraction.

One more push and the resident told me it was time to do an episiotomy. So I took scissors and cut the posterior vaginal opening to enlarge it. I was taught to do this procedure because it would be better than having a hard-to-heal tear from the baby's head. (Episiotomies were common at the time, the early 1980s, but decreased in frequency by the 21st century after studies showed they didn't provide the advantage doctors thought.) The baby slid into my hands—as did a lot of amniotic fluid and blood. The baby was slippery. I held him tight.

"It's a boy!" I announced. "Congratulations." The mother was crying—emotional tears, hopefully of joy.

A nurse handed me a clamp for the umbilical cord. I clamped the cord in one place, and then slid my fingers along the cord to move blood out of the way, then clamped in a second place. The nurse then handed me another pair of scissors, and I cut the cord between the two clamps. "Thanks for stripping the cord," she said. (They hated it when the delivering doctor let the cord blood get all over the place.)

I handed the slippery, crying baby to the nurse, who took him over to the side of the room to clean him off. "Apgar score 10, I think. Good pulse, healthy cry, good color," I said. The nurse concurred and brought the baby to the mother to hold.

Then we waited for the placenta to be delivered. I sewed up the episiotomy, the resident watching over my shoulder.

"Nice job," he said.

"Thanks for letting me take the lead," I replied.

About five months later, three weeks before my due date and feeling big as a house, a contraction woke me up. I looked at the clock—six a.m.

Bruce was getting ready to go to his fellowship. "Can you wait a bit? I'm having some contractions. Could be nothing, but just in case."

I felt another contraction. It'd been seven minutes.

"Let's take a walk around the block and see how I feel," I said to Bruce. While walking, we timed the contractions—five minutes, then another one in five more minutes, and again five minutes later. They were steady, regular—every five minutes. Time to go to the hospital.

They put me in an examining room and told me the resident would come to check me.

"Who's the resident?" I asked. "What's his name?"

Of all things—it turned out it was the same resident that was my supervisor during my OB-GYN rotation!

"I'm sorry, but I do not consent to that resident examining me. I need my doctor," I said.

The nurse rolled her eyes, then left to call the doctor. I told Bruce, "I am NOT letting that sexist, racist resident touch me!"

When my doctor arrived, he examined me and told me I should go home—it was three weeks before my due date, and, since was my first baby, it would take a while.

But I knew it was time. I just knew. I said I didn't want to go home, and my doctor kindly let me stay.

Five hours later, with Bruce by my side during my labor, help-ing me with the breathing (huff, huff, huff, huff; we had taken the Lamaze class together), and no sedative for the excruciating pain (I turned it down), and no episiotomy (the doctor said he'd only do an one if absolutely necessary), there she was: our baby daughter, Lauren! "This is where everybody cries," the doctor said, and tears flowed from all our eyes.

The nurse dried Lauren off and started to take her over to the side of the room to put her under a heat lamp. But the doctor said, "Give her to her mother to warm up," and so I warmed her little naked body against my bare skin, Bruce there the whole time—our new family. I was lucky to be in a comfortable birthing room and not in a separate delivery room (birthing rooms in hospitals being a new idea in the early 1980s) and having a natural childbirth.

We stared at our tiny baby. We counted her fingers and toes (ten of each!), and we fell in love with her. And the next day, we took her home—in a car seat, of course!

A few weeks later at home, I looked down at the face of my beautiful baby girl, Lauren, as she cried her head off while I held her in my arms, rocking her back and forth. It was bedtime, but she wouldn't stop crying. When I held her, she cried. When I rocked her, she cried. When I laid her in her crib, she cried. I picked her up to console her. She quieted for a moment... then she cried.

"She must be tired, why won't she go to sleep?" I asked Bruce. "What do you think we should do?"

"Well, we've fed her, changed her diaper, swaddled her in her blanket, rocked her, comforted her. I don't know what's the matter," he said. "Too bad she can't tell us. If only she could talk."

"Hmm... crying and not sleeping are behaviors. Did I ever tell you about the experiments I did in college about pigeon behaviors? Pigeons can't talk either." So I told Bruce the story about training two pigeons in my college psychology laboratory (which I told earlier).

"I had unintentionally rewarded the naïve pigeon for turning his head!" I told Bruce. "Do you think picking up Lauren is unintentionally rewarding her for crying and not sleeping?"

"Could be," he said. "Let's try not picking her up."

The next evening, after feeding, changing, and swaddling Lauren, I laid her down in her crib. She cried. I left her room and closed the door. She cried. I went into our bedroom down the hall. She cried. I closed our bedroom door to dampen the crying sounds. She kept crying.

I put my hands over my ears. Bruce put his arms around me. "Don't go in to her," he said, holding me back. Finally, after two hours, she stopped crying and was asleep. "Whew, I'm glad that's over," I said.

I looked at the clock. It really had been only ten minutes. The next night, it was five minutes. The following night, two minutes. Then, for the next 18 years, Lauren went to sleep without crying (as far as I knew). Our son, Don, born two years later, was easier because we knew what to expect.

As Lauren and Don grew up, we tried not to reward unwanted behaviors, as I had with my second pigeon (that I trained to be neurotic). And we tried to reward good behaviors with positive reinforcement, as I had done with my first pigeon.

Bruce and I didn't always remember to reward good behaviors, which meant we gave intermittent positive reinforcement, which, as I had learned from my pigeons, is very effective. But we weren't diehard behaviorists. We were interested in what our kids were thinking—when they finally could tell us (after they graduated from college).

Lauren and Don are grown now, and they turned out great. Although, when I told him the pigeon story, Don said that when he's hungry... sometimes he turns his head to the side.

Three months after Lauren was born we found a nice Pakistani woman, who had two older girls, to take care of Lauren during the day so I could go back to my training. She was the wife of someone Bruce knew from the school of public health. Sometimes I cried when I left Lauren off in the morning, but they treated her like a member of their own family, hugging and kissing her when I brought her over in the morning and picked her up in the evening.

Three months didn't seem like enough time to be with her, but it was all I could get. I had to go back and finish my residency. Later, when Don was born, I took nine months off to be with the kids—luckily, I was between jobs then. It was almost like we planned it.

Checking Boxes

After only four years of medical school, medical students have learned enough to be awarded an MD degree and take a licensing exam to practice medicine. Three more years of additional training after medical school, as a resident, qualifies them to take a medical board exam in a specialty field, which opens the door to setting up a medical practice. In 1981 I was finishing up my family practice internship. I would need two more years as a resident if I wanted to be board eligible in family practice.

The last rotation of my internship was inpatient internal medicine in a private hospital affiliated with the medical school. Our team had patients on different floors, an unusual situation. Every morning, I put a blank sheet of paper on a clipboard and listed each of my patients, the top floor first, then each floor below in turn. I drew a square to the left of each patient's name, and after each name I listed tasks. When I completed all the tasks for a patient, I checked off the square. This was my daily "TO DO" list. Here's an example of a list for a typical day (but there were 20 to 25 patients on it):

☐ 15th floor: J Tempkin – congestive heart failure: check blood electrolytes, check blood oxygen level, order chest X-ray

☐ 15th floor: D Jones – renal failure: check blood creatinine, request urology consult

☐ 14th floor: J Finkelstein – type 2 diabetes mellitus: check fasting blood sugar

But this is closer to the way I would have written it:

☐ 15 Tempkin CHF—✓lytes, ✓blood O2, order CXR

☐ 15 Jones renal failure—✓creatinine, urology consult

☐ 14 Finkelstein T2DM—✓FBS

I still make lists with boxes to the left of each item to check off. Sometimes I put an item on the list that I've already completed, so I can immediately check it off to give me a feeling of accomplishment. [Format memoir manuscript—check.]

After morning rounds with our team, I took the elevator up to see my patients on the 15th floor, then I walked down the stairs, stopping to see my patients on the 14th floor, then the 13th floor, one floor at a time until I finished on the lowest floor. One by one, I checked off each box on my To Do list.

I asked each patient how he or she was doing, did a targeted exam (examining just the problem area), looked at test results, ordered new tests when needed, ordered or discontinued medications as needed, did minor procedures (like reinserting an IV that had infiltrated) and, when the patients were ready, wrote discharge orders. I documented it all by writing SOAP notes on their medical charts.

By afternoon rounds, I could report to our team on every patient. "Tempkin—CHF is better, lungs clear, O2 level good, 'lytes back to normal, on dig and diuretics. He wants to go home, so I say OTD [Out The Door]."

Although I consulted with doctors who had more experience, for most patients I knew what tests to order and what the results meant, how to make a correct diagnosis, and what treatments to prescribe. Perhaps more importantly, I could relate to the patients, listen to their problems, and understand their concerns. But now it was time to decide whether to move into my second year of family practice residency, or whether to concentrate on preventive medicine and public health.

I thought about my patients: Mr. Harris, my first patient, died of metastatic cancer from smoking. Alice, the teenaged girl with Type 1 diabetes, was in repeated comas because she didn't give herself insulin. Mr. Burch had heart failure because he hadn't gotten antibiotics for strep throat when he was a child. Mr. Bud drank until his liver stopped working. Ms. Jones was taken off a medicine because the attending physician didn't know about new evidence or didn't believe it mattered.

All these situations could have been prevented!

I thought about public health: Social conditions and health behaviors are important for good health. We can improve people's health by improving environments. We can do studies to identify risk factors that can be reduced to prevent diseases.

And I thought about my personality. I preferred to delve into a problem and spend some time on it, rather than seeing a patient every fifteen minutes. I could work in an area that could help whole groups of people at a time. And I enjoyed the science of epidemiology—finding what exposures increase the risks of disease.

So I decided not to do the next residency year in family medicine, but rather to concentrate on preventive medicine and public health as my specialty.

When I told a classmate about going into preventive medicine, he asked jokingly whether that meant I would stand outside the ER and keep people from coming in! But someone I met at a party wasn't joking when he told me I had wasted one of the rare spots in medical school because I wasn't going to see patients—because instead, I was going into "preventative medicine." I never considered that he could possibly be right. And what did he know anyway? He even got the name of the specialty wrong! (It's preventive, not preventative.)

My next step was to finish my preventive medicine residency. I didn't know it at the time, but I had decided to concentrate on a field perceived by medical schools and research funders as less important than basic science conducted in a laboratory and clinical science conducted on patients who already were sick. I would have supervisors, including physicians in leadership positions, who, like most medical students, weren't taught much about concepts I would learn, internalize, teach, and believe in.

PUBLIC HEALTH/PERSONAL DISEASE

Causal Evidence

"I brought you something," Dr. Sherwin said, folding his lanky frame into one of the desk chairs in the windowless residents' office where I was sitting by myself at one of three metal desks. He was a professor in the department of epidemiology and preventive medicine, where I was doing my preventive medicine residency in 1982. After completing the MPH program at Hopkins and my last rotation in family practice, I was spending a year in his department for hands-on training in the field.

"In the 1960s, they were looking at whether smoking causes lung cancer," he told me, in his professorial British accent. "Sir A.B. Hill came up with a way to consider the evidence. I brought you a copy of his seminal paper." The paper, published in 1965, was called *The Environment and Disease: Association or Causation?* "I thought we should talk about it and maybe consider teaching it in the redesigned course."

Dr. Sherwin had asked me to help him redesign the epidemiology course that the department taught to second-year medical students. In the current course, a lecturer provided facts like "blacks have more hypertension than whites" and "older people get more strokes than younger people"—descriptive epidemiology about the distribution of diseases. This information does help you recognize horses, not zebras, when you hear hoofbeats behind you (as Dr. Woodward had us imagine), but it doesn't give much information about what causes disease or about public health approaches. I had taken that course; it was a yawning bore. They did need to change it.

Hill's paper posited that just because there is an association between an exposure and a disease, it doesn't mean the exposure causes the disease. As an example, the prevalence of radios in the U.S. dramatically increased during the same period that the mortality rate from cardiovascular diseases increased (circa 1920-1950s)—the two were correlated (or associated). But that doesn't mean radios cause cardiovascular mortality. By listing types of evidence that could lead one to conclude that an exposure causes a disease, Hill's list formed a foundation for analytic epidemiology.

[For causes of infectious diseases, we use Koch's Postulate, which states that a microorganism "causes" a disease if it is present in every case, can be isolated and grown in culture, and reproduces the disease when delivered to a susceptible host.]

I found Hill's evidence of causality to be a useful conceptual model for the rest of my career. To summarize Hill, the more of these "criteria" that exist, the more likely the exposure actually causes the disease:

  • *Biological plausibility*—Though specific biological mechanisms may not be known, it makes biological sense that the exposure in question could cause the disease.
  • *Measures of association*—Exposure is statistically associated with disease in population groups.
  • *Consistency across studies*—Findings are similar in multiple studies.
  • *Biological gradient or dose-response relationship*—The higher the exposure level, the higher the disease rate.
  • *Temporal sequence*—The exposure comes before the disease.
  • *Specificity*—If you control for other factors, the association persists (I changed Hill's meaning; this makes more sense to me).
  • *Coherence*—The association is consistent with other knowledge.
  • *Experimental evidence*—If you increase (or decrease)

the amount of exposure, the disease rate increases (or decreases).

Using the example above, the prevalence of radios and rate of cardiovascular mortality, though associated, clearly has no biological plausibility and does not meet most of the types of evidence. A causal relationship between elevated blood cholesterol and cardiovascular mortality, however, meets all the criteria in the list.

The following week, Dr. Sherwin came to see me again (his office was in another building, but he came to the main building regularly.) "What did you think of Hill's paper?"

"It's interesting. We should teach this stuff to the medical students."

"I was thinking the same thing. But medical students aren't interested in such things."

That was a constant problem with our field—the vast majority of medical students were interested in individual patient care, not in the health of populations.

"Do you think we could make it interesting?" I asked.

"I should ask you that. You were a medical student recently."

After some thought, he asked, "What about the medical literature? Don't doctors need to read the literature to keep up in their practices?" He was talking about peer-reviewed articles of scientific studies published in medical journals.

"Do they already have any classes on how to read the literature?" I asked.

"No. I don't think so." He mulled it over, stroking his beard. "I have lots of published papers we could use. Cohort studies, case-control studies, randomized trials."

He was talking about the three major study designs we could teach to the students, which are seen often in the medical literature. (As you recall, I had first learned about these designs from Dr. Gordis at Johns Hopkins.)

"The papers are about CVD risk factors," he added. Cardiovascular disease was, and still is, the leading cause of death in the nation and had received a lot of attention in epidemiology and prevention research.

"So…maybe they could learn three things in the course: how to read the medical literature, epidemiology study designs, and how we know about cardiovascular risk factors," I concluded. "And maybe we could sneak in Hill's level of evidence."

"The curriculum committee wants us to use more small groups in classes. We could have them read the papers and then discuss them in groups."

Now we had a plan: We would teach epidemiology to medical students by having them read published scientific reports of studies that use different types of study designs, and then discuss those papers in small group sessions.

Dr. Sherwin compiled the original papers from the medical literature that would serve as the course's "textbook." These papers told the story of cardiovascular disease prevention.

One example is the story of hypertension: Case-control studies had observed that people who had strokes had, on average, higher blood pressures than similar people who hadn't had strokes. Then the Framingham study, which was an observational cohort study, found that higher levels of blood pressure were associated with higher rates of stroke later in life; this finding resulted in high blood pressure being dubbed a "risk factor" for stroke in the 1970s. After that, the Hypertension Detection and Followup Program (HDFP), a randomized trial published in the late 1970s, found that lowering elevated blood pressure reduced the rate of strokes. Other randomized trials confirmed this finding.

We taught this series of studies because they showed the progression of research from observational studies (case-control and cohort studies—which do not test any interventions to change a presumed risk factor) to randomized trials (which determine the effects of interventions that change—generally reduce—the presumed risk factor). That is a typical study progression providing a high level of evidence. This series of studies also illustrated Hill's evidence of causality: these studies showed an association, a dose-response relationship, the correct temporal sequence, and experimental evidence that lowering elevated blood pressure reduces rates of cardiovascular diseases.

Dr. Sherwin enlisted other department faculty to help teach the course in small groups. A pair of instructors—an epidemiologist and a statistician—led each group.

I was paired with a statistician and taught one of the groups. I wasn't a card-carrying epidemiologist, as I didn't have a PhD in epidemiology. But those were rare, even on the faculty. Many epidemiologists were physicians who had learned epidemiology methods (or cynically "doctors who can count").

The students read the journal articles, and we taught them what to look for—research question or purpose, study design, and details like dropout rate and analysis approach, as well as the findings and conclusions. We said, "Don't just read the abstract"—which is the summary of the paper at the beginning. (Though I confess, sometimes I do just read the abstract.)

Our students learned so well that they soundly criticized every single study—even the landmark randomized trials, which provide the highest level of evidence! Since there is no such thing as a perfect study, by the end of the course we had to unteach the students just a little bit, so they would believe things that they read.

At last, my residency training was over, and I was ready, at the age of 32, for the first real job of my career. Bruce had finished his postdoctoral fellowship in behavioral medicine, so we looked nationwide for a place that had jobs for both of us.

After many interviews where there was either something for him but not for me, or vice versa, we found a place where we both could get a good job: Galveston, Texas, where there was a huge medical complex.

We had no family there—no grandparents, aunts, uncles—no support system. But we put our careers first and decided to go to Texas, with our two-year-old daughter, Lauren, and our in-utero son, Don.

Our son was born in a Texas hospital, where they wheeled me to a separate delivery room, wanted to cut an episiotomy (I did not consent), and snatched my baby away before I could hold him. Bruce followed the nurse who took baby Donnie down the hallway to the hospital nursery, and he stayed there until they finally let me have my baby in my room hours later—but only because I was a doctor!

So our two-career family with two small children settled in Galveston, Texas, where cockroaches flew and were as big as birds, you had to watch out for fire-ant hills when you walked, we had to board up the house nearly every year because of potential hurricanes, and there were four seasons, but three of them were summer.

TELLING PEOPLE

"I'm glad you're here," I say, having just walked into the living room of our condo apartment in Maryland. My husband, Bruce, is there with two of my three sisters, who are in town to help get our Mom's house ready to sell because she moved to assisted living. My third sister has just gone back home to Boston after helping.

"You know I've been having some problems with my arm and hand." My sisters had been giving me little massages of my stiffened muscles around my left shoulder blade, to loosen them up.

"I've been to a neurologist. I want to tell you what he said."

I paused. How do I say this? I guess I'll just say it.

"I have Parkinson's Disease."

They look shocked—we are all shocked. Everybody stands up, and we all hug and cry.

That evening, I call my two grown children, Lauren and Don. I don't want to wait until I see them; I have to tell them right away. They both sound very concerned, but they seem to take the news pretty well. It reminds me of when my dad called to tell me his ALS diagnosis—I was about their age. I had no idea about what to expect for my dad then—nor for myself now.

I call my other sister who lives in Boston and tell her the diagnosis. She sounds concerned. "How are you doing?" she asks.

(Devastated, shocked, worried.) But I reply, "Not too bad. I just need to get the right treatment."

Bruce wants to talk about my condition with a friend at his work. I worry that if someone at his work knows, word will spread to people I work with because he also works at NIH, though in another institute.

Would it be disruptive at work if people knew? Would they treat me differently? When people have heart attacks, their work colleagues often know. When they have surgery, or breast cancer, or other medical problems, their work colleagues often know. This isn't different. Or is it? I'm not sure. People may have more misconceptions, or little knowledge, of rare conditions like Parkinson's.

I think about it a lot and decide that I don't want to add any more issues to my already difficult job, but I do decide to tell my deputy, Karen, because if my condition gets worse, she may need to take over. I also tell my supervisor in case something happens, and I need reasonable accommodations or extended sick leave. My supervisor thanks me and seems very supportive.

Bruce keeps my secret at work, but he says he's not good at keeping secrets. (That's true.) I tell him to think of me as Clark Kent. (Or Wonder Woman?) But we do tell a few friends who all seem surprised and concerned. Some of them ask about details—symptoms, tests, and medications. It helps me to talk about it. I start writing it all down.

"I'm not sure I should tell my mother," I say to Bruce one evening. My mother is 95 years old. "She had to endure Dad's ALS. She'll worry all night and not sleep—night after night. That's the kind of person she is—always has been."

Every time I think of telling her, I start to cry. I decide she doesn't need to know; I don't want her to be miserable in her last years because of me. Before he died, my father asked me to take care of my mother. One way to take care of her is not to tell her about my condition.

But I think about what she was like before her stroke. She would walk shuffling her feet, bent slightly at the waist, looking like she was about to fall over even when she used a walker. And she has a tremor. Does she have it too? But I don't do anything about this notion. She already had seen a neurologist for her tremor, who said it was nothing. But I know more now. Should I take her to another neurologist?

Even if she has it too, I'm not sure it would make a differenc life. She's barely mobile as it is and happy in her new assistec apartment.

I meet an old friend for lunch. Her mother died of Parkinson's. I tell her about my diagnosis. She is visibly moved. She tells me that her mother died of pneumonia caused by aspiration of her own saliva because she couldn't swallow. That's similar to how my dad died of ALS. I can't help but think that might be the way I go too.

I don't feel normal. I'm pretty sure I'll never feel normal again. My left leg aches, my left arm is stiff, my left hand shakes and is uncoordinated. I feel anxious all the time. I feel wobbly when I walk. I get in bed, fully clothed, pull the covers up to my chin, and weep.

PART 5: CAUSES AND PREVENTION

"If we want more evidence-based practice, we need more practice-based evidence."

—Lawrence Green, Ph.D.

It's All About Behavior

I t was 1984. The nation re-elected Ronald Reagan as President in a landslide, Michael Jackson released *Thriller*, researchers discovered the AIDS virus. And five of us on the faculty of the School of Allied Health Sciences at the University of Texas Medical Branch in Galveston, Texas (Guy, Bruce, John, Kathy, and me) were in a conference room discussing what to include in a grant application to the Centers for Disease Control.

Guy, both Bruce's and my boss for our new jobs in Texas, chaired the meeting. "The purpose of this grant," Guy told us, "is to identify evidence-based strategies that health departments could use to prevent chronic diseases in their communities. And to write handbooks with the information and guidance for local health departments."

Handsome with a full brown beard and smiling with dimpled cheeks, Guy was soft-spoken, but he knew how to get things done. He had asked us whether we wanted to apply for the CDC grant. He knew the answer before he asked us—of course we wanted to apply—but I appreciated being asked instead of being told.

"We need to think about what health departments could do to prevent chronic diseases in their communities," Guy said. "Of course, they should educate people about healthy behaviors, but what else should they do?"

"Let's use PRECEDE as a framework," said Kathy. PRECEDE (Predisposing, Reinforcing, and Enabling Constructs in Educational Diagnosis and Evaluation) was developed by a leader in health education and promotion, Dr. Larry Green. The framework was used widely in the field. "PRECEDE says we should consider not only internal factors, like knowledge, but also external influences, like environments. Both are important," Kathy continued.

"I agree we should include environments. If a person is constantly exposed to inexpensive food high in calories and portion sizes, for example, you can't say it's her fault that she's obese," John said. "That would be blaming the victim."

Guy and Bruce had been working on an approach to promote heart health in schoolchildren. It included curricula to teach students about healthy diet and exercise. At the same time, it changed the school environment to be healthier. The cafeteria served healthier foods and PE classes were more active.

"School is one of four settings CDC identified as an important environment for health," Guy said. "The other settings are worksites, healthcare institutions, and communities. We should use those four settings."

"Schools, like other organizations, create local environments. Like what to serve in the cafeteria," Bruce said, "through school policies and programs."

"Yeah, policies and programs of organizations are important," John added. "So are laws and regulations. For example, laws require stores to keep cigarettes behind the counter and not sell them to kids. And studies show that higher cigarette taxes may reduce teen smoking."

As the junior person at the meeting, I was taking notes. So I summarized, "We talked about different settings—the four settings from CDC. But it seems we also have different levels—like a hierarchy. People whose health we're interested in, environments within organizations where those people spend time— schools, worksites, communities—and governments that have laws and regulations."

"So we have three levels—individuals, organizations, and governments. And we have four settings—schools, worksites, healthcare institutions, and communities," Guy said. "Let's discuss whether each level is relevant to each setting."

We brainstormed what organizations could do in the four settings to create healthier environments: serve healthier food in cafeterias (school setting), establish no-smoking policies at workplaces (worksite setting), encourage doctors to advise patients about health behaviors (healthcare institution setting), develop parks in neighborhoods to promote physical activity (community setting).

And we brainstormed what governments could do to improve environments: school boards could require PE, counties could pass laws banning indoor smoking at worksites, cities could change zoning for parks, the federal government could allow Medicare to reimburse healthcare providers for educating patients about health behaviors.

"Those are great examples. I'm sure we can come up with a lot more!" Guy said. "But could health departments influence organizations?"

"Getting programs and policies in place," Bruce said, "is what decision-makers do. The manager, or principal, or CEO, or whoever makes decisions in an organization."

"So we aren't just interested in behaviors of people whose health is of concern," I said. "We're also interested in behaviors of decision-makers who shape the environments."

And so a multi-level model for action was born. To help people be healthier, teach them about healthy behaviors, but also create healthy environments by influencing decision-makers to make health-promoting changes in environments—like policies and practices. We used the terms "target population" for the people whose health was of concern, and "targets of intervention" for the people you need to influence to create healthy environments.

Kathy spoke up, "It's a good concept. But we should use PRE-CEDE for the handbooks—it's famous. Everybody uses it. Why should we use something new?"

"I think the multi-level model would work well," I said. "It uses a classic public-health concept of improving environments to improve health."

Kathy and I argued back and forth about which model to use. Then Guy said, "That's enough discussion. We're going to use the multi-level model." Good, a decision (and a good decision), I thought.

All models need a name, and we came up with the acronym "MATCH," which stands for Multi-Level Approaches Toward Community Health. It's a good acronym because the model is about matching the type of intervention to the level you are trying to influence. And it's pronounceable.

"I have good news and bad news," Guy told us months later at a staff meeting. "We got the CDC grant! But now we have to do the project!"

Our team was to write three handbooks for health departments—one a year. That was an ambitious project. "They want us to start with physical activity. CDC just reviewed the literature on physical activity and health. There was more evidence than they realized."

"Denise," he said, "you'll be responsible for writing the literature review sections. Susan, you can be in charge of finding examples of programs and policies around the nation, and Kathy, please work on a needs assessment and evaluation section." (Susan recently had been hired, and John and Bruce were busy with other projects.)

Guy, the CDC folks, the rest of our team, and outside consultants fed me citations for scientific papers on the topic, and I started a huge drawer full of reprints (no pdfs of articles yet). I learned to summarize the literature in evidence tables—a row for each study, columns for things like citation, study subjects, interventions, measurements, findings.

Guy had bought the entire faculty IBM desktop PCs that used 5.25-inch floppy discs. Using WordStar, I summarized information from the evidence tables. When I completed a draft, I had to see what I wrote in black and white on paper (maybe because the computer had green letters on a black background!). So I printed it out, using a dot-matrix printer with continuous-feed paper that had holes on the sides to feed it through the printer. A chapter would take a while to print, so I would write all morning and then let the printer run when I went to lunch. "I know when you're at lunch," Guy told me, "because I can hear your printer printing." After lunch, I removed the perforated edges, separated the pages from each other, and read the latest version, only to find things that needed editing.

Steve, a big name in physical activity epidemiology, and Carl, who worked on national surveys about physical activity at the CDC, were our consultants. About forty observational cohort studies had found that more physically active people have fewer heart attacks and live longer than less active people. Other studies, including randomized trials, found that physical activity improves fitness, blood pressure, blood cholesterol, body weight, and other health parameters. The message was clear—physical activity is important for your health.

But that information doesn't tell us what health departments could do to promote physical activity. Does teaching a person about physical activity result in them becoming more active? Does providing more parks result in higher physical activity levels in a community? Do worksite flextime policies result in higher physical activity levels in employees? Though these were logical assumptions, they also were researchable questions. But studies to answer them were lacking.

We discussed this situation at a meeting with our consultants. Steve said, "There's no evidence for these strategies. You can't make recommendations without evidence."

We sat and stared at each other, wondering what to do next. Then Carl spoke up. "We need to make the best recommenda-

tions we can, even if the evidence is sparse—or nonexistent."
And so Carl unstuck us and provided a philosophy I would use
later in my career: make the best recommendations you can
from the available evidence.

Susan connected with various people around the U.S. to
collect information about programs, policies, or regulations
that seemed successful, or maybe just promising. One example
is the Rails to Trails Conservancy, which built trails in communities. Kathy created a needs assessment strategy to estimate
the problem in local communities as well as an evaluation
approach. She used PRECEDE in her sections. But the primary
model was MATCH, which worked great for the handbooks.

The project also worked great for us. Susan started a walking
program, and I started jogging (well, wogging—alternating
walking and jogging). I exercised regularly for the rest of my
life. Though we didn't say it in the handbook, I concluded that
one way to get people to be physically active is for them to
write a book about helping people become physically active!

The MATCH model was a great idea. I thought so then, and I
think so now. But when we tried to publish a paper about it in
a journal, our paper kept getting rejected. Journal editors told
us that it was nothing new. We finally got a paper published in
1988, but in a minor journal without much reach.

Though we were told it wasn't new, MATCH actually was one
of the first "ecological models" that included multiple levels of
environmental influences on health—an idea whose time had
come. Various people developed other ecological models over
the next couple of decades. Some were published in high-profile
journals.

MATCH was unique in that it offered strategies for changing
environmental exposures—by influencing decision-makers
to implement healthful programs, policies, and practices. The
influences could be top down or bottom up, or a combination.

I used the underlying concepts behind MATCH for the rest of my career. And Bruce and Guy used it in textbooks they wrote about health promotion.

DENISE SIMONS-MORTON

Who's Pushing Them In?

"A man and a woman are picnicking by a river," I said into the microphone on a podium in a huge lecture hall at the start of my lecture to 200 medical students in 1984. I now had a faculty position in the medical school in addition to a position in the school of allied health sciences. "They see a body floating down the river—a man, calling for help. They jump in, pull the man out, and save his life. Then another body floats down the river. They jump in. This time they save a woman. More bodies float down the river. The picnickers save as many people as they can. But they are so busy pulling bodies out, that they don't have time to go upstream... and see who's pushing them in."

I paused and scanned the faces in the audience.

"Your other classes are about pulling bodies out—helping people who already have a health problem. This class is about what happens upstream, preventing the problem in the first place, keeping people out of the river."

I was lecturing to second-year medical students for a course on preventive medicine, which I taught from 1984 to 1987 at the University of Texas medical branch in Galveston. This course, as most preventive medicine courses at US medical schools, had substantially fewer hours on the curriculum than other classes, like anatomy and microbiology. It wasn't considered a core class, and faculty and students often didn't take it seriously. There were no guidelines on what medical stu-

132

dents should learn about prevention and public health (there were only a few questions on the medical licensing exam), so I decided to teach them what I wished someone had taught me when I was in medical school.

"This course covers preventing disease before it occurs—called primary prevention. It also includes early detection of disease before there are symptoms—part of secondary prevention. Preventing subsequent episodes of a disease, like a second or third heart attack, is another part of secondary prevention. Tertiary prevention is about preventing adverse outcomes from disease through rehabilitation.

"A lot of disease prevention is through environmental approaches. Here's a slide that illustrates that concept—it shows mortality rates from TB in the UK over time," I said.

Remember when I was in medical school, Dr. Rocky (a radiologist, of all people) had closed the classroom door to tell us the "truth" about medicine? Now I had a slide showing what he had drawn on the chalkboard. I had looked up and plotted the TB mortality rates for different years, putting a little arrow at the year the tubercle bacillus germ was discovered (1882 by Robert Koch), adding a bracket showing the period where germ theory was developed in the 1800s, and putting another little arrow at the year antibiotic treatment for TB started (1944, when streptomycin was first used).

"TB mortality decreased during this entire time, before they even knew about germs and well before they had antibiotics to treat it. So how did this reduction occur?" I asked rhetorically. "Cities cleaned up waste, people stopped throwing waste out of their windows, nutrition improved because of better agriculture and refrigeration."

My message was the same as the message that had introduced me to public health years before. The environment is important for health! We can improve environments by individual action (like stop throwing your garbage out the window), and also by societal action (like setting up city sanitation systems).

Clearly, I was auditioning—the students would decide, based

on this first lecture, whether to keep coming to my class. Looking over the sea of faces in front of me, I wondered if any of them was interested.

"Today we're going to talk about screening," I started the lecture for the next class, pleased that a fair number of them had returned. "Who knows what we mean by screening?"

No one raised a hand. I showed a slide with a definition of screening and explained, "Screening is testing people who don't have symptoms so you can discover and treat a disease early —before the person would normally seek care—for example, removing a small cancer before it has a chance to spread. Screening is a major part of secondary prevention—identifying disease early in its natural history.

"To determine how good a screening test is you calculate its sensitivity and specificity," I paused. The students were doodling, passing each other notes, resting with their eyes closed. Perhaps sleeping.

Maybe I should bring some screening (you know, like for a screen door or window—from a hardware store) to introduce the topic of this class. Because it was, you know, about screening! That at least would be funny. Maybe. But I pushed on.

I gave them the following terms and asked the class what they meant, calling on those who raised their hands:

- True positives (people who test positive and have the disease)
- False positives (people who test positive but don't have the disease)
- True negatives (people who test negative and don't have the disease)
- False negatives (people who test negative but really have the disease)

Then I had an idea—I asked for two volunteers. Pointing to two students sitting in the closer rows, I said, "You and you, please come to the front of the room." They arose, looked around, shrugged their shoulders, and walked up to the front of the room. "Please take a piece of chalk." They found pieces on the ledge below the big chalkboard that stretched across the front of the lecture hall.

Then I and gave them some specific numbers so they could calculate the values for:

- Sensitivity (proportion of people with disease who are positive on the test)
- Specificity (proportion of people without disease who are negative on the test)

We discussed key take-home points: That there is often a tradeoff—a test may have either high sensitivity or high specificity, but usually not both. You would want sensitivity to be high if the disease is very serious, so you don't miss anybody that has it. But high sensitivity often has a lot of false positives. You should not base a diagnosis on a screening test alone. Rather, a screening test should indicate when you need to do further testing.

As you probably realized, screening is not simple. Issues about test characteristics (sensitivity and specificity), availability and cost of screening tests and of treatments, and how much and what type of evidence is needed all come into play when deciding what screenings should be done and in whom. These issues lead to differences of opinion, some of which we shall get into later.

Threats To Health

Though the lecture hall held 200, only about 30 medical students attended on the day in 1985 when I told my preventive medicine class that smoking and unhealthy diets are the two biggest threats to our nation's health. I wanted them to think about the big picture—the entire nation, not only the patient sitting across from them. I noticed there was a student note-taker in the front row, so the missing students could read the notes.

"In 1900 the top three causes of death in the U.S. were infections: Influenza or pneumonia (counted as one disease), tuberculosis, and gastrointestinal infections," I told them. "Today, the top three causes of death are chronic diseases: heart disease, cancer, and cerebrovascular disease (strokes). This shift in causes of death was primarily due to better control of infectious diseases along with an increase in chronic diseases —especially through the first half of the 20th century. Diet and smoking are major causes of the increase in chronic diseases.

"Imagine waking up this morning and hearing or reading that two jumbo jets had collided mid-air. Each plane had 500 people on it, and all 1,000 passengers died. You'd be shocked, wouldn't you?

"Now imagine waking up tomorrow and hearing that another collision occurred—everybody dies, two days in a row. It would be unprecedented! Then the next day, another crash... and every day for a month, the same type of crash—a thousand people dead every day from airplane crashes!"

I paused, looking out at the sparse class.

"Wouldn't there be an outcry?" I asked. "The nation would rally to get these crashes to stop!" Some were nodding.

"Well, that's how many people die from smoking! About a thousand people a day, every day—350,000 to 400,000 people every year." I loved this analogy, which had been spreading through the field.

"How do we know that smoking causes lung cancer?" I asked. "Studies in humans show 10 to 25 times the risk of getting lung cancer in people who smoke compared to people who don't smoke. This magnitude of relative risk is rare. Most studies of risk factors look for about a 20% higher risk, not ten times the risk! And there are a huge number of animal studies showing that smoking is harmful. What should we do about this public health problem?"

I told them that behavioral counseling could help, but it's not always successful. The most successful quitters are people who have tried multiple times, relapse, and finally succeed. Tobacco is addictive, so stopping smoking requires a lot of motivation.

"There's some evidence that doctors giving patients simple advice to stop smoking helps increase cessation rates, though a single doctor would have a hard time noticing the effect without counting a lot of patients. So ask your patients if they smoke, and if they do, advise them to stop!"

The smoking rate in the nation increased in the 1950s, peaking at about 40 percent in the 1960s, and then dramatically decreased to below 20%, where it is today. The reason for the decline doesn't seem to be because doctors are advising their patients. That has helped, of course, but there's been a major cultural shift in societal norms and policies, like smoking bans in public buildings.

But I didn't think of talking about policy to my class even though I was working on handbooks for health departments that included environmental change through policies. I didn't think the medical students would be interested in policy, so that's why I had talked about what doctors could do with individual patients.

More recently, the U.S. Preventive Services Task Force, an expert panel convened by the government to assess evidence and provide recommendations, advised clinicians to use the 5-A system: Ask, Advise, Assess, Assist, and Arrange:

- *Ask* the patient if he/she smokes.
- *Advise* the patient to quit smoking.
- *Assess* the patient's level of willingness to quit.
- *Assist* the patient by providing smoking cessation resources, such as cessation materials or referrals to counseling, nicotine replacement therapy, or other help.
- *Arrange* follow-up visits or phone calls to monitor progress and provide additional assistance.

And I'll add: use your prestige as a physician to influence policy.

"Today we have a guest lecturer," I announced the following week. "Dr. Frank is an obesity expert. He's going to talk with you today about obesity."

Dr. Frank walked up to the podium and faced the class. "Obesity is an important health problem. But what can we do about it? Well, there are several different diets: a low-fat diet, a low carbohydrate diet, a high protein plus high-fat diet, even a grapefruit diet.

"Do these diets work?" he asked the class. "Sure, they all work."

What? I cringed. My guest lecturer was telling the medical students that all diets work! His statement was misleading. Diets may work, but if they do, it's usually short-term, and a lot of the early weight loss from any diet is water. He probably just forgot to say that diets work short-term only. But I didn't invite him back the following year.

Why don't "diets" work? If you want to lose weight and maintain the loss, you need a permanent change in your dietary patterns, not a temporary "diet." You need to eat healthful foods, in moderate-sized portions—forever. Adding exercise helps, but the energy expenditure side of the equation has been over-promoted. Let's say you want to lose weight through a daily calorie deficit of 150 calories. It's a lot easier for many people not to drink that 150-calorie soda than it is to walk for the 30-40 minutes it takes to expend the same number of calories.

Obesity is an even bigger problem today than it was then. Obesity prevalence started to increase dramatically pretty much about the time Dr. Frank lectured to my class in the early 1980s. (I don't think this was a causal relationship.)

Years later, I became an internal spokesperson for obesity research at the National Institutes of Health. By 2012, about two-thirds of adults were overweight or obese, with half of those obese. Obesity is associated with higher rates of heart disease, diabetes, hypertension, some types of arthritis, and a variety of other health conditions. It's a major public health problem that has the possibility of undoing decades of improvement in the nation's cardiovascular health. Losing just five to ten percent of your body weight can improve your health, mainly by improving risk factors like high blood pressure.

I jumped on the obesity bandwagon at NIH because of the broad interest in the topic. But I was also interested in the effects of diet and physical activity for reasons other than obesity.

Diet and physical activity affect blood pressure, blood cholesterol, insulin resistance, and a variety of other parameters even without a change in body weight. So don't believe the myth that diet and physical activity are only relevant when it comes to weight.

What Is A "Cause"?

We need to know what causes a disease to prevent it. Epidemiology studies have identified many causes of disease that are commonly accepted today. For example, high blood pressure causes strokes and high blood cholesterol (especially the "bad" cholesterol called LDL) causes heart attacks. These causal relationships are not deterministic; they are probabilistic. In other words, not everybody with high BP will have a stroke, not everybody with high blood cholesterol will have a heart attack. But high BP and high blood cholesterol increase the risk, or probability, of getting the disease.

"Sir Austin Bradford Hill provided a list of things to look for when we want to find out if an exposure causes a disease," I told my class while projecting a slide with this list:

- Association: The exposure is associated with the disease.
- Temporal order: The exposure comes before the disease.
- Dose-response: The higher the exposure, the greater the disease risk .
- Consistency: The association is seen in multiple studies.
- Specificity: The association persists when controlling for other exposures. [Note: I changed Hill's meaning.]
- Biological plausibility.
- Experimental evidence: If you change the exposure, subsequent disease rates should change.

I told my students that we can get this information from three basic study designs (which I learned from Dr. Gordis and

Dr. Sherwin):

> • A *case-control study* compares past exposures in people who have a disease with similar people who don't have the disease.
> • A *cohort study* compares future disease rates in people exposed to a possible cause with people not exposed to the possible cause.
> • A *randomized trial* is an experiment that compares disease rates in people who get an intervention with people who do not get the intervention.

Each of these basic epidemiology study designs can provide different types of causal evidence, as shown in the scheme below, which I created for the purpose of teaching:

Evidence of causality	Case-control study	Cohort study	Randomized trial
Strength of association	Yes	Yes	Yes
Dose-response relationship	Yes	Yes	Yes
Temporal order	Possibly	Yes	Yes
Specificity (control for confounders)	Incompletely through matching and statistics	Incompletely through statistics	Yes through randomization
Experimental evidence	No	No	Yes

As you can see, randomized trials can provide information about all of the items of evidence. That is why randomized trials are said to provide the highest level of evidence. Randomized trials, however, are complex and expensive; we need sufficient evidence from prior observational studies to warrant conducting a randomized trial.

Using examples of studies from the cardiovascular field (which I had gotten from Dr. Sherwin), I described the three study designs and the points about causal evidence. One of the studies was the Hypertension Detection and Followup Program (HDFP)—the randomized trial that had resulted in me treating Mrs. Jones for high blood pressure in my family practice clinic and that Dr. Sherwin and I had included in the medical school course.

"For an exposure to be a cause of disease, there has to be an association with the disease—the first item on Hill's list," I told the class. "One measure of association—perhaps the most important—is the relative risk. Does anybody know what we mean by 'risk'?"

A young man raised his hand, and I called on him. "That's easy," he offered. "Risk is the probability of getting a disease. It is measured by the proportion of people who get the disease."

"Correct. It's an estimate of the probability of getting the disease, obtained by analyzing data from many people. Risk is a percentage—a probability. And relative risk is the ratio of one risk to another risk. To get relative risk, we divide the risk in one group by the risk in another group—say risk of getting a stroke in people with high blood pressure divided by risk of getting a stroke in people without high blood pressure."

"So what does a relative risk of 1.0 mean?" I asked rhetorically. "That there is no excess risk," I answered. "A relative risk of 1.5 means there's a 50% higher risk. And a relative risk of 10 means there is ten times the risk in one group compared with another group."

There may be sufficient evidence to conclude that an exposure is one cause of a disease, but it's probably not the only cause. For example, high blood pressure, high cholesterol, and smoking all are causes of heart disease. As are genetics and family history, male sex, having diabetes, being overweight, and being sedentary.

In observational studies (case-control and cohort studies), we can isolate exposures we are interested in through analyses that statistically control for many exposures simultaneously —assuming we have, in fact, measures of them. In randomized trials, the process of randomly assigning people to receive or not receive an exposure (or intervention), balances out all the other exposures so the only difference between groups, on average, is the exposure (intervention) you are testing. That is, if you have enough people randomized. (To figure out how many you need, consult a biostatistician.)

When I was teaching the preventive medicine course, about two students every year told me they found it interesting. Many of the other 198 medical students gradually stopped coming to class; attendance usually ran at about 20-50.

The students seemed more interested in what they should do for the patient sitting across from them than in population health. But I hoped they read the notes from the note-taking service and that I was getting through to them about the importance of population and prevention thinking. And that they at least would understand relative risk when they read a published paper.

Do I Belong Here?

I loved teaching preventive medicine to medical students, but not everybody loved that I was doing it. I heard that an assistant professor in my department, who had a PhD in epidemiology, was saying that I wasn't qualified to teach the course. Maybe she had wanted to teach it herself, but I had been asked to do so by the department chairman. In retrospect, if I had thought of it at the time, we probably could have taught it together.

One day a faculty member in my department asked me to consult about a case-control study being planned. As you recall, in case-control studies the researchers try to identify risk factors by looking into the past to see if they can identify exposures that are more common in people with a disease (the cases) than in similar people without the disease (the controls). They find out about patients' pasts by interviewing them or their families or looking at medical or other records.

I went to my colleague's office to discuss the study. She wanted to know about symptoms of heart failure. Okay, so I knew about heart failure. How could I not? It was a common reason for patients to be in the hospital, and I saw it frequently during my training. But I wanted to work on study methods—what research questions to ask, how to identify the cases, how to identify the controls, what data to collect, what analyses to do. She could have found out about symptoms from a textbook. I asked her some of those methods questions, but she was only interested in discussing symptoms with me.

Another faculty member in my department asked me to join his study team, and I was delighted. It turned out that he wanted me there when study participants had fitness tests on a treadmill—I was supposed to do CPR if something happened. I don't know why I wasn't included in discussions about the research—the study purpose, design, methods, interventions, measurements, analyses.

So my faculty colleagues seemed to want to work with me as a physician, but not as a research colleague—probably not surprising as they were PhDs and I was the only MD in the department. And I was being accused of not being qualified to teach the medical-school course in my area of specialty. They didn't seem to know why I was there, and I began wondering myself. I wanted to do research, but I didn't know how to get started. I should have been on a senior researcher's study, not just for the medical issues, but also to learn how to do research and to get grant funding.

I needed a mentor. Or lacking one, I needed more training in how to conduct research. So after three years on the faculty of a school of medicine, I arranged to take a postdoctoral fellowship in health promotion research starting in 1987 at the University of Texas School of Public Health in Houston.

After commuting for a year to Houston from Galveston, we moved our household to Houston, where there was not only a school of public health but also a huge medical complex that included a couple of medical schools and a lot of opportunities for my career, and for Bruce's.

REACTION

I can't stop crying. I'm devastated about my diagnosis of Parkinson's Disease.

I think about how hard it was helping my dad when he suffered from ALS and gradually lost the ability to walk. I learned to transfer him from his bed to his wheelchair: he would sit on the side of his bed as I stood facing him. Bending my knees so I wouldn't hurt my back, I would lower myself to his level and give him a big bear hug. Holding him tightly, I would stand up, bringing his thin body with me, all five feet five inches of it. Then I would pivot—his legs dragging, useless—and set him down in his wheelchair.

Will I get that way too? Who will transfer me?

My physical therapist tells me about an episode of Larry David's show "Curb My Enthusiasm." He says Michael J. Fox, who has Parkinson's, was on the episode; that the show was irreverent and funny.

I locate the episode on demand and watch it with Bruce. Michael J. Fox comes on—he is uncoordinated, moving his head side-to-side, walking strangely. He mumbles, and I can hardly understand him. I remember him clearly from when he was young—I saw the "Back to the Future" trilogy at least four times. Parkinson's disease really changed Michael J. Fox.

I don't want to get like that. I can barely watch it…. but I just can't turn it off. I also watch him later on "The Good Wife" and a new sit-com in which he starred (which was cancelled). It's remarkable that he's still acting.

I'm not hungry. I start a meal feeling hungry, but then feel full really soon and lose interest in eating. It seems impossible to eat the quantity of food I used to eat.

I lose weight. My shoulder bones protrude because the muscles between my shoulders and neck have atrophied. But at least I can now wear my "test pants"—the pants I try on to decide whether I need to lose weight.

Speaking of weight, here's a story about my weight: When I became a vegetarian and stopped eating meat, I lost five pounds. Later, when I stopped eating candy and desserts, I lost five pounds. Then when I stopped drinking calories and only drank diet drinks, tea, or water, I lost five pounds. And lastly, when I started exercising regularly, I lost five pounds. The thing was, they were the same five pounds. [Pause for laughter.] But all kidding aside, now I lose 15% of my body weight—20 pounds. I feel like I'm wasting away.

Our grown daughter, Lauren, calls to see how I'm doing. I'm in bed, with the covers over my head. Bruce hands me the phone. I tell her that I'm hanging in there. I start to ask her if she and her husband plan to have children—it has become more important to me now to have grandchildren. I start crying and hand the phone to Bruce. "I can't talk; you talk to her." So I refrain from asking either of our grown and married children about possible grandchildren, knowing I will just cry.

Of course, they need to have kids when they are ready, not when I'm ready. But I wonder whether I will have grandchildren before I become so incapacitated that I can't play with them, lift them up on my lap, and tell them stories. Stories like the one about a bird in the woods—a story I made up when my kids were small:

The Bird in the Woods

Once upon a time, there was a little girl named Lauren and a little boy named Don.

They lived in a house with their mother. It was near the woods. They would go for walks in the woods and look for birds in the trees.

One day Lauren and Don were walking in the woods. They saw a blue bird up in a tree. It was singing, "tweet tweet tweet, tweet tweet tweet."

They went to see it every day. Every day they heard it sing, "tweet tweet tweet, tweet tweet tweet." They fell in love with the blue bird.

They told their mother about the bird. Their mother said, "Why don't we catch the bird and bring it home to live with us?" Lauren and Don were so excited. They loved the idea.

So their mother bought a birdcage. She put some birdseed in the cage. They took the cage to the woods.

They saw the bird. It was in the tree. It was singing, "tweet tweet tweet, tweet tweet tweet." They set the cage on the ground and opened the door. They stepped behind a tree and hid. They waited.

The bird came close. He tilted his head. He looked like he was thinking. He looked inside the cage. Then he went inside.

The mother came out from behind the tree. She closed the cage door. She had caught the bird!

Lauren and Don were so happy!

They took the cage home with them. They put the cage upstairs in Lauren's room so she could keep the bird company. She loved the bird and was glad he was there.

The next day the bird wasn't singing. The mother said, "Let's bring the bird to the kitchen. It is very sunny there. Maybe then the bird will sing."

They took the birdcage to the kitchen and put it in a sunny corner. But the bird wouldn't sing.

And now the bird wouldn't eat. The bird wasn't happy. It started losing its feathers.

"What should we do?" asked Lauren.

"Well," said the mother. "I think we need to take the bird back to the woods."

Lauren and Don were sad. But they understood. The bird needed to be in its own home.

The next day, the mother went with Lauren and Don to take the bird in its cage back to the woods. They set the cage on the ground and opened its door. They stepped away to give the bird room.

The bird hopped to the door of the cage, looked around....and......and... flew up to the top of the tree.

Then it started singing, "Tweet tweet tweet. Tweet tweet tweet."

The bird looked happy again. Don and Lauren were so happy that the bird was happy.

They took the cage home and put it away. They didn't think they would use it again.

They were happy that the bird was back in its home. And that it was happy too. And they went to visit the bird every day. And listened to it sing.

Tweet tweet tweet. Tweet tweet tweet.

PART 6: HEALTH BEHAVIORS, HEALTH CENTERS

"Science isn't a tall stack of hard facts: it's a difficult and deeply human process that lurches toward an approximation of the truth."

—Joel Achenbach, Science Reporter, the Washington Post [July 23, 2014]

Patient Education

When I started my post-doctoral fellowship in health promotion research in 1987, in Houston, Texas, I met with Pat, who would be my supervisor. She was a behavioral health researcher with a lot of research experience.

We went out with Ellen, her other postdoc, for a snack and talk. Wearing a tan jacket, just a tad lighter than her light brown shoulder-length hair, and a colorful silk top, she leaned back against the side of the booth and, taking her time, talked about several things she was working on—some of which I didn't understand.

She told us about conducting a meta-analysis. "That's a study of studies," she explained. "A kind of study where you combine results from multiple previous studies on the same topic. I want to look at whether patient education and counseling delivered in clinical practice actually improves health behaviors. And I'd like you two to help me."

It was just the kind of research I was interested in—the effectiveness of interventions for prevention, directly relevant to clinical practice. What people should do to be healthy is one question; how to help them do it is another question—a researchable question. This would be my first real research project working with a senior researcher.

"That sounds interesting," I said. "Some doctors think they're powerless to change patients' health behaviors. Others think all they need to do is give out pamphlets. It'd be good to know what works."

"Maybe doctors don't think pamphlets actually work," Ellen said. "They just want something easy, so they can feel like they're helping."

"We're not only interested in what doctors do," added Pat. "Don't forget nurses and nutritionists. Health educators. Physician assistants. Everybody that's part of the healthcare team."

"And patient package inserts," added Ellen. Ellen had been studying whether inserts that pharmacists give with prescription medications help improve adherence to medications.

"We're going to look at all the behaviors recommended by the USPSTF," Pat told us. The U.S. Preventive Services Task Force was a panel of experts appointed by the federal government to make recommendations for preventive care based on the available evidence. "And I'm going to bring in an expert to train us all in meta-analysis methods."

Does patient education and counseling work to improve health behaviors? It sounded like a simple question—and one we should already know the answer to. But it actually was very complicated, and the answer was unknown. The USPSTF recommended nine health behaviors: condom use, breast self-exams, physical activity, injury prevention actions (like wearing seatbelts or helmets), healthful diets, stress management, not smoking, limiting alcohol intake, and controlling body weight. Later, some of their recommendations were modified, and some added, as more evidence accrued.

"We have a lot of behaviors to look at—it's a bit overwhelming," Pat said at one of our meetings, "so let's think about grouping them into categories of behaviors. Possibly combining them is as different types of behaviors, conceptually."

"Exercise and wearing seatbelts are healthy behaviors people should add," I offered.

"For weight loss, you need to subtract calories eaten and add calories expended," Ellen added.

"Hmmm…." Pat was thinking. "Whether behaviors are additive or subtractive—could be a good approach. Subtractive behaviors could be substitutive—substituting something else for the behavior. Like substituting healthy foods for fatty snacks."

"Smoking is about subtracting a behavior that's addictive," Ellen offered. "Maybe addictive behaviors should be in a different category than other subtractive behaviors."

Pat seemed excited about the direction the discussion was going. "Maybe we could have three groups of behaviors rather than nine individual behaviors."

"Let me see if I've got this. Subtractive or substitutive would be one group, subtractive but addictive would be another, and additive would be the third?" asked Ellen.

"Yeah," Pat confirmed. "Hmmm… that would result in one group about nutrition and weight loss, another group smoking and alcohol, and a third group a bunch of additive behaviors like exercise, seatbelt use, and using condoms."

If we grouped the behaviors into three categories, we could conduct three meta-analyses (one for each group), rather than nine meta-analyses (one for each behavior). It would make the project doable. So we proceeded with this plan.

Next, we needed to find all the published studies that addressed the question. Pat instructed us: "They have to be studies about health behaviors for primary prevention (patients without disease). They have to test an intervention to improve at least one of the nine target behaviors. The intervention needs to be delivered in a clinical practice setting. The studies need to have a control group that receives no intervention or a different intervention. And they need to have measures of behavior change in both the intervention and control groups."

Pat had a research assistant run an electronic search of PubMed (an online library of medical journal articles) for potentially relevant citations. The search included the paper title, authors, journal name, and abstract, which is a summary of the article. Ellen and I were to go through the list separately to find relevant studies. If we agreed a study met our inclusion criteria, then it was included. If we agreed that it did not meet the criteria, then it was excluded. If we couldn't decide, we would look at the whole paper, not just the abstract. If we disagreed, we needed to discuss it and come to a mutual decision. If we still couldn't decide, we would take it to Pat for her to decide.

"Did you get through the first 200 citations?" I asked Ellen about a week after we started going through the list.

"Yeah," she said. "Most of them aren't even studies—they're opinion pieces or review papers. And others are observational studies that didn't test an intervention."

"I saw that too. I also saw a lot of exploratory analyses that didn't compare intervention and control groups to each other." Laughing, I said, "I thought there were a lot of LPUs!"

A "least publishable unit" (LPU), is a joke term about people taking just one small piece of a study and publishing it, then another small piece and publishing it separately, until they had numerous published papers from one study to help their academic credentials. "Publish or perish" as they say.

"Let's go through the list of includes and excludes," Ellen said. "Remember, Pat said to count the citations and keep track of how many are includes, to find out the percent."

After weeks of work, we had looked at about 5,700 abstracts and obtained and read about 600 papers. Of these, 74 studies had tested about 100 interventions (some of the studies had more than one test intervention). This was a yield of about 13% of the original citations, which is a pretty high percentage for this kind of work. We published two separate papers on our process and the yield—not LPUs (we didn't think so!), but papers that gave more detail so we could reference them later in the main result paper.

"Patient education and counseling can be done in a lot of different ways," Pat told us. "I want to compare intervention approaches to see what works best. Let's create a list of possible characteristics of interventions." Using prior work Pat had done, our list included whether the intervention was only in writing or included interpersonal contacts; how many contacts there were; whether the intervention used behavioral approaches or not; and other characteristics.

We created an abstraction form to record all the relevant information from each study, including the findings. Pat had other staff input the data into a database, and then a senior statistician analyzed the database to combine the results of all the studies. The analyses teased out characteristics of the interventions to compare their effects on the study outcomes.

Did we find out whether patient education and counseling worked? Yes, we did. The answer was yes. The interventions, on average, significantly reduced smoking rates, improved measures of nutrition and weight loss, and improved additive behaviors like exercise and seatbelt use, compared to their control groups. So all three types of behaviors were significantly improved. That is not to say that the interventions worked for every patient; we were interested in averages for the group.

What kind of approaches worked best? Just giving a brochure with information didn't work. Though that's what many people do, it didn't surprise me that a brochure didn't work because it's tough to change behaviors. For instance, I never could get Pigeon number two to stop moving his head to the right.

Behavioral approaches worked better than other strategies: Self-monitoring (for example, keeping a food diary to see if you're reducing your calories to lose weight), individualized goal setting (like how many minutes of exercise you plan to do tomorrow), engaging others to give social support (like asking your spouse to come on a walk), and problem solving (like asking your spouse why he won't come on a walk).

Using more than one communication channel worked better than using only one communication channel, for example, using written materials, video, and personal counseling all in the same intervention program. In many of the successful interventions, a doctor gave advice, and a nurse or someone else on their team provided counseling.

Surveys had found that most doctors don't believe they can influence patients' health behaviors, but based on these results, we concluded that they could—if they or their staff would do more than just having pamphlets in the waiting room. And for years afterward, I would say, along with others, that information is necessary but is not sufficient for behavior change.

I learned something in this project—not just about what types of interventions work or how to do a systematic review and meta-analysis, which I did learn (and which came in handy later in my career). I also learned something else: Don't ask complicated questions because they are difficult to answer.

Unfortunately, I had to relearn that later—because I still kept working on projects that asked complicated questions. Maybe that was because I was interested in applied studies that are directly relevant to the real world, conducted with living, breathing, and unpredictable human beings.

And one thing about the real world compared with a laboratory is that it's complicated.

Moving The Target

D r. Annegers stroked his chin, staring at the floor as he
stood at the front of the classroom. With short brown
hair and glasses, wearing a sports jacket with suede
patches on the elbows over a collared shirt with no tie, he
looked to be the typical professor. He took his time before
answering questions—always pausing, sometimes stroking
his chin. I was a student in his class on advanced epidemiology
methods, which I took in 1988 during my postdoctoral fellowship in health promotion. The course focused on analytic epidemiology methods used to identify risk factors for disease.

What started the chin-stroking that day was a student
asking: "I don't understand about adjusting for multiple comparisons. Can you explain it?"

Researchers do a lot of analyses in observational epidemiology studies—studies that look at naturally occurring
exposures and diseases without testing the effects of any
intervention, like the case-control and cohort studies I mentioned previously. The purpose of the analyses is to look for
associations—for example, whether smoking is associated
with lung cancer. The goal is to find associations unlikely to
have occurred by chance and thus more likely to have occurred
because of a real relationship—like maybe smoking causes lung
cancer.

Scientists typically calculate a p-value (probability value) to
assess whether an association is significant. A p-value less than

0.05 is generally used to call something "significant"—meaning there's less than 5% probability that the result occurred by chance alone. To control for multiple comparisons, say three comparisons in the same dataset, you wouldn't say the association is significant unless the p-value was less than 0.05 divided by the number of comparisons; in this case, 0.05 divided by 3, or 0.017. So adjusting for multiple comparisons makes it harder to get a significant result.

Dr. Annegers explained all this and concluded: "If you adjust for multiple comparisons," he continued, "there has to be a big effect to say something is significant. So you aren't misled into saying things are important when they aren't."

The student replied, "But Dr. Rothman says in his book that you don't need to adjust for multiple comparisons." Dr. Rothman—the dentist epidemiologist who wrote a whole book about epidemiology methods, which we were using as our textbook. I met him several years later. Nice guy. Smart.

"I think you should adjust for multiple comparisons, but others, like Rothman, disagree," replied Dr. Annegers. "But everybody agrees you need to describe what you did when you write it up. So others can interpret what you found."

Later in my career, I found out that pretty much nobody adjusts for multiple comparisons when analyzing data from observational epidemiology studies, where the purpose is to generate hypotheses to be studied further. But for randomized trials, where the results will directly affect medical care, you want to be sure you're right when you say there's a significant effect. So most researchers identify a single primary outcome (like mortality), when designing a trial and don't have to adjust for multiple comparisons. If they are interested in two primary outcomes (like the incidence of stroke and of cancer), they would adjust for two comparisons.

I sat in the front row in Dr. Annegers' class and asked a lot of questions—I wanted to understand everything. They must have been good questions because he asked me to be his teaching assistant for the following year. The way to really learn something is to teach it, so I agreed.

Next year, he asked me to present the topic of "interactions." Using transparencies and an overhead projector (no Power-Point yet), my lecture went something like this:

"Let's say we look for an association between an exposure and a disease," I said, putting up a transparency that had one solid line indicating low-to-high exposure from left to right on the horizontal axis across the bottom, and another solid line indicating low-to-high disease rates from bottom to top on the vertical axis on the left. A dashed line went from the lower left to the upper right, in the space between the axes. I had made up this graph to illustrate the concept.

"This graph shows that the higher the exposure, the greater the disease rate. But let's say these are data only in women."

I put another transparency on top, which had a dashed line going from the upper left to the bottom right, so the two dashed lines crossed each other—an exaggeration to illustrate the concept.

"What if the association in men goes the opposite direction, as shown here—the higher the exposure, the lower the disease rate. We have an interaction: sex interacts with the relationship between exposure and disease. We also can say sex is an *effect modifier*—sex modifies the effect of the exposure on the disease." I liked the term 'effect modifier' better than the term 'interaction' because I thought it was clearer.

"Why is interaction important?" a student asked.

Dr. Annegers had to answer the difficult questions—the students were really smart. But I could answer this one. "If there's an interaction and you combine the data—men and women together—you wouldn't see any association: the direct association in women and the inverse association in men would cancel each other out, leading to incorrect conclusions." (This topic reminds me of the joke my dad used to tell: if half of a person is in boiling water and the other half is in ice, on average the person is comfortable.)

I continued, "Doing analyses in different types of people—in this case by sex—gives you a more accurate picture. You also can look at other subgroups, like race or age."

"When should you look at subgroups, and when do you not need to?" the student asked.

"Dr. Annegers, can you comment on that?" I punted.

"It's a good idea to have a reason to look at subgroups before you look," Dr. Annegers replied. "A reason like findings from prior studies or biology. You should ask a question of the data, not analyze data to see what pops out. But if you do decide to see what pops out, please say so, and don't make a big deal out of what you found. Also, keep in mind the issue of multiple comparisons. The more subgroups you look at, the more comparisons you are making, and the more likely you'll find something just by chance alone."

Actually, many researchers do look at data this way and that way, upside down and right-side up, to see what "pops out" (unflatteringly called a fishing expedition). So a lot of findings are spurious and don't mean much of anything. That doesn't stop journals from publishing the results, however, nor does it stop the press from reporting on new findings. But it's why you have to look at an entire body of evidence—not just a single study—to get an accurate picture.

There were a lot of concepts in this epidemiology class that I used every day for the rest of my career. It was much more complicated than the basic epidemiology I had taught to medical students. Here are two things I learned that are important and may interest you:

We can conduct analyses to examine several exposures at the same time regarding their relationship to a single outcome. For example, we could estimate the risk of getting a heart attack based on a person's blood pressure level, cholesterol level, age, sex, and smoking status. Results provide effects of each exposure controlling for all the other exposures at the same time.

We can calculate a 95% confidence interval, which means we are 95% sure that the true measure of association (such as relative risk) is in between two numbers. For example, a relative risk of 1.5 (people exposed are 50% more likely to get the disease than those not exposed) could have a confidence interval of 1.2 to 1.8. The true relative risk is somewhere between those numbers.

I needed to learn these things because I now was working toward getting a Ph.D. in epidemiology. My interest in science finally was being fulfilled—an interest I had since creating a notebook of the animal phyla, seeing streaks of droplets in a cloud chamber, doing an experiment with frog eggs, and training a pigeon to peck a key (and become neurotic, turning his head repeatedly, because I screwed up shaping his behavior).

When my coursework for the Ph.D. was over, I passed a qualifying exam enabling me to move on to the dissertation phase. It would take me a while, however, before I got that Ph.D. The paid portion of my fellowship was over, and we had two children now. I would have to work on my dissertation while I had a job.

I'm The Boss?

I n 1989, I walked into an outer office at the Baylor College of Medicine in Houston, Texas. Each of three desks was occupied by a secretary. One secretary was moving slides from plastic storage sheets into a slide carousel, another was sorting slides on a lightbox, and the third was talking on the phone. I waited until one of them looked up. "Can I help you?"

"I'm Dr. Simons-Morton, here to see Dr. Vallbona."

"I'll buzz him and let him know you're here," she said, picking up the phone.

Dr. Vallbona appeared a moment later in the doorway between this reception area and his office. "*Buenos dias*, Denise. Come in, come in," he motioned for me to enter. He was about 20 years older than I was, short and wiry, with a lot of energy.

I looked around the office. Floor to ceiling bookcases were crammed with books. He gestured for me to sit down facing his large desk as he moved to his seat across the desk.

"I'm glad you're here. I've been looking at your CV. Very impressive."

"Thank you. Can you tell me about the position?"

"*Si*. This position is for Assistant Professor at Baylor. The main role is in the community health program," he spoke rapidly. "Part of the Harris County Hospital District. Provides care to medically indigent community residents—no health insurance or other ways of paying. Funded by property taxes. Patients pay on a sliding scale depending on what they can afford."

"Sounds interesting," I said. "So what would my duties be?"

"You'd be my deputy. Oversee medical staff at five community health centers around the county. A medical director and a half dozen or so doctors, physician assistants, nurse practitioners at each center. A total of about 50 medical staff."

"So the program combines clinical care with public health?"

"*Si*, a good way to think of it. But you would not see patients. You would oversee the functioning of medical staff."

Why did he think I was qualified? It must have been my Hopkins training—maybe the course in healthcare administration I took. And, of course, my medical training. "It sounds like an important job."

"*Si*, these people are needy. Best system in the country, helping people like this."

"I'm very interested in that. It's why I went into public health."

"*Bueno!*" He smiled and leaned back in his chair, putting the tips of his fingers together.

"What else do I need to know?"

"Baylor provides medical staff. Hospital district provides other staff—nurses, lab techs, pharmacists. They take care of infrastructure—buildings, appointments, medical records, labs. You won't have to worry about any of that. You'll just be responsible for medical staffing. Make sure we have coverage when anybody's out or leaves—we've had vacancies lately." An understatement, I learned later.

"Might there be time some to do some research?"

"*Si*. You could work on research halftime. The District can give you data from the system that tracks patients. *Serio bueno* to do some research in the health centers. Lots of interesting things to look at."

"Can I go see health centers before I decide how interested I am?"

"Sure." He buzzed one of his three secretaries. "Please ask Granville to contact Dr. Simons-Morton for a health center tour. ... Great. Thanks."

Then, turning back to me, "Granville would be your physician assistant. He can give you a tour whenever you can arrange it."

So I met Granville, who had served as a medic in the Vietnam War and had parlayed that experience into becoming a physician assistant. (He taught me not to add an "s" to the end of "physician;" it's not physician's assistant). He took me on a tour of a couple of the health centers. They were interesting, busy places. Waiting rooms packed with people. Children crying or sucking their thumbs on their mamas' laps. Old men with canes, hunched down in their chairs. I met the medical directors and some of the docs while I was there. Highly dedicated people, making a difference.

I was offered the job and took it. The work was important. And I thought I would even get some research done. Dr. Vallbona didn't tell me, although I learned later, that the "half time" he mentioned for research only would be possible if I worked 120 hours a week.

A few months later I was in my new office when Granville stuck his head in the door. "The docs wanna know if they can leave early because of the Thanksgiving holiday coming up."

"I don't know, can they?" I asked.

"Up to you. You're the boss," he replied. I looked up at him; he looked back at me, nodded his head, and smiled. "What do you say, boss?"

This is going to take some getting used to, I thought. "Okay. They can leave after the patients are seen."

"Yes Ma'am. I'll let them know." And he saluted me!

I relied on Granville —he knew so much about how the system worked and the people in it. I would have been lost without him.

Most of my day-to-day work in the Hospital District was making sure we had adequate medical staff—calling in back-up care when a doctor was unexpectedly out, interviewing and hiring replacements when doctors left. We were always short-staffed. It seemed like every time I turned around a physician left to take a job in the private sector.

The docs had to be really committed to work in the setting of a community health center—relatively lower pay, patients who arrived three hours late because of cultural differences in appreciating appointment times, patients who didn't speak English (Spanish was more common), patients who hadn't seen a doctor in a while so their health problems had worsened.

The lobby of the nearby private hospital looked like an upscale hotel—lush plants, light streaming from a glass roof over a high-ceilinged atrium, a reception desk of marble with a receptionist offering help. The lobby of the District hospital, on the other hand, looked like the government building that it was —bland off-white paint, no plants, no high ceiling, no streaming light. Just narrow, dull beige hallways with peeling paint and cheap metal chairs. And the salaries mirrored the differences. Where would you rather work?

So I was constantly looking for qualified medical staff, with ads out all the time. I hired everybody who walked into my office that had a license to practice medicine—especially if they were board certified. I hired physician assistants and nurse practitioners as often as physicians. We managed to cover patient care, but it was hard and stressful. And it wasn't my only responsibility.

A lot of patients came to the Emergency Room with minor problems that didn't require emergency care. The health centers were well suited to providing care for many of the problems, and the ER needed its resources for true emergencies.

So I worked with Hospital District administrators, hospital

doctors, and our health center doctors to develop a policy where the ER would triage patients with minor problems to the health centers on weekdays when the centers were open. We developed a list of specific problems for which the triage was allowed: colds, sore throats, mild diarrhea, earaches, splinters, etc. Patients stayed at the ER for things like chest pain, abdominal pain, stroke symptoms, broken bones, or other potentially serious problems.

The policy was a major success. Even the patients liked it—they could be seen more quickly at a health center than waiting in a busy ER. The medical director of the ER was delighted, as was Dr. Vallbona, who told me the hospital loved me. I knew that was because I helped them get what they wanted. I didn't have any turf issues. It just seemed like the right thing to do.

But things didn't always work that well. One day, I got a call from the Hospital District administrator for the community health program. Like many healthcare administrators, she had been trained as a nurse. Dr. Tristan, a medical director in one of our health centers who devoted his career to helping the downtrodden, and some other doctors, felt like they were working for nurses—a situation they didn't like. Dr. Tristan referred to them as "the nurse cabal."

"Would you have a problem with your health-center docs seeing pregnant women for problems not related to their pregnancy?" the administrator asked me after I answered the phone. At the time, pregnant women were not seen at the health centers; they needed to go to the hospital obstetrics clinic.

I was pulling together some papers for a meeting and didn't have much time to talk, so I thought for a brief moment and said, "Well, that may be all right, I guess, as long as the docs wouldn't take care of the pregnancy." I imagined the docs seeing pregnant women for things like colds or sprained ankles. "We don't have OB-GYNs, and only a few of the family medicine docs see GYN patients."

"Thanks," she said and abruptly ended the call, clearly not interested in talking much.

I expected, though didn't ask, that this was just an idea that, if they were serious, would be worked out with input, like the ER triage policy had been. But the very next week, the District released an official policy saying that pregnant women were to be seen in the health centers for problems unrelated to their pregnancies!

It was an extrapolation of the ER referral policy, in a way. But I felt blind-sided. They must have already written the policy, with it ready to go, when she called me. And she used my brief reaction as an approval to go forward. I had no chance to run it by my docs.

My docs were livid! And they were right. "Everything about a pregnant woman has to do with her pregnancy," Dr. Tristan told me. "Because every medication can affect the fetus. There goes the nurse cabal again!"

I spent hours and hours doing damage control—trying to get the District to modify the policy. They changed a few specifics about which health problems to exclude, but I felt I had let my docs, and the patients, down.

When I had started in the position, I believed my job was to collaborate with District administrators to ensure the patients were cared for appropriately. But by the end of a couple of years, I thought my job was to protect my medical staff from the administrators, so the docs could take care of the patients as they saw best.

When the District came up with a rule that the community center docs needed to see 25 patients a day, for example, I pushed back. Unsuccessfully. And the docs were furious. ("Those damn bean counters," said Dr. Tristan.)

Unexpected events occurred frequently. For example, one of our doctors had forged the date on the renewal of his state medical license, which we discovered doing a routine review of our files. (We could see erasures!) All he had to do was pay for his license renewal, but he let that slip. Since he had been seeing patients without an active license, I had to fire him. It was a shame; he was a good doctor.

Our docs also provided well-child care at the health department once a week. One day absolutely nobody was available to go. I went myself, and, because I wasn't used to doing this job, afterward I kept thinking about things that I missed.

So, although Dr. Vallbona told me I was doing a great job, I was pretty sure I was in over my head. Constantly needing to assure coverage in the clinics, never knowing what issues might arise, dealing with organizational politics, every morning I had to tell myself, *You can do this job! You can do this job!* so I could go out the door to work. I really needed to finish my Ph.D. dissertation... so I could move on to a job more suited to me.

I worked on my dissertation after hours and during holidays. To this day, I have no idea how I managed everything—a full-time stressful job, analyzing data and writing a dissertation, two toddlers in daycare. Childcare was a constant stressor; some mornings, I sat in my car and cried after I dropped the kids off. But I wasn't going to give up—I deserved a professional career the same as a man, the same as my husband, Bruce, who shared taking care of our children and the household.

In my preventive medicine residency, I had worked with some of the faculty collecting data for health-services research about emergency services. Because I already had the experience of collecting data, I got permission to analyze those data for my dissertation. And so the University of Maryland kindly sent me the dataset.

Interested in how science can inform the real world of health care, my research question was this: in patients with penetrating injuries (gunshot or stab wounds), does being treated at a designated trauma center, compared with being treated at a general hospital ER, result in lower mortality?

This question followed the four parts of a clear, answerable research question: (1) in whom, (2) what intervention (or exposure), (3) compared to what control (or comparison), (4) on what outcome? The format is also called PICO for short, which stands for Population, Intervention, Control (or Comparison), and Outcome.

I did the analyses myself on a laptop computer using multiple logistic regression, a method to control simultaneously for multiple factors. Survival (yes/no) was the outcome. Since more severely injured patients often are taken to trauma centers rather than to general ERs, to make the proper comparisons between type of treatment center, I needed to control for injury severity. I also controlled for other things, like patient age, sex, race, systolic BP, location of injury (chest/abdomen), and ambulance transport (vs other transport). My dissertation was a good example of using epidemiology methods to answer a health-services-research question.

What did I find? The trauma centers did not have lower mortality than the ERs after controlling for other variables. It was an interesting finding but not a definitive one because the patients weren't randomly assigned to a trauma center versus general ER care.

Although I did get a paper published about data sources for penetrating trauma, I never got the main findings published. I wrote and submitted a paper for publication, but I didn't persevere in revising it and resubmitting it as is usually necessary. I was just too busy. And worried about controversy the findings could produce. But I did get the degree.

So in 1992, after three years at Baylor and the Hospital District, and after obtaining my Ph.D. degree, I was ready to move on.

Two job opportunities were open at the National Institutes of Health—one for me and one for Bruce—and we took them. I left a job I believed in but hated. Bruce left a job he really liked, but in a model egalitarian fashion, he agreed to leave so I could find something better.

We packed up our family and moved back to where I had grown up, where most of my family still lived—parents, grandmother, uncle, several cousins, and one of my sisters—to the suburbs of Washington, DC, where Bruce and I both would work at the National Institutes of Health.

MEDICATIONS

*I*t's 4 a.m., and I'm up, working on my computer. I popped up out of bed wide-awake about an hour ago.

It's been like this for months since I was diagnosed with Parkinson's Disease. I wake up after only four hours of sleep. I don't know if it's the Parkinson's or the medications. I don't spend the extra awake time on my office work—I'm already working more than 40 hours a week at NIH—but I've gotten a lot done on my writing and my artwork (I've been doing digital "paintings") and reading about Parkinson's.

Parkinson's treatment focuses on reducing the motor symptoms —the stiffness, rigidity, tremor, uncoordination, and problems with balance. About a half dozen classes of medications are available, and there are many possible combinations. But none of the medicines offers a cure or has been proven to delay disease progression.

Parkinson's occurs because of a lack of dopamine in the brain. Dopamine is a neurotransmitter—a chemical made by the body that sends signals from one nerve to the next and from nerves to muscles. The failure of nerve signals to get transmitted adequately results in the movement problems of Parkinson's .

After diagnosing Parkinson's, my neurologist prescribes Sinemet, which is a combination of levodopa and carbidopa. Though a lack of dopamine is the problem, giving dopamine as a medication doesn't work because dopamine doesn't reach the brain—it's stopped by the "blood-brain barrier." Levodopa, a precursor to dopamine, however, does go through the blood-brain barrier, and it's converted to dopae in the brain. Adding carbidopa helps keep the levodopa from converting in the periphery where it is ineffective. The carbidopa also decreases nausea that many people have when taking levodopa.

I start Sinemet the day Dr. Satinsky makes the diagnosis—about three months after my fall. Three times a day, immediately after each dose, nausea sweeps over me. It feels like a stomach virus. I run to the bathroom, go down on my knees in front of the toilet, hold onto the sides of the toilet seat, and throw up.

If I can keep the medication down, my symptoms improve, but four or five hours later, the medicine wears off, and the symptoms come roaring back, stronger than before. I'm on a miserable roller coaster, alternating between being nauseous but without Parkinson's symptoms, and being symptomatic with bothersome rigidity, uncoordination, stiffness, and tremor, but no nausea. Perhaps the Sinemet is too strong; the doctor says to try a half dose, so I cut the pills in half. But I still have the roller-coaster effect. Dr. Satinsky prescribes a controlled release version of Sinemet, which takes longer to break down, but that only helps a little.

So we try drugs from other classes. A drug called rasagiline (Azilect) inhibits the enzyme that breaks down dopamine—it's in a class of medicines called Monoamine Oxidase Inhibitors (MAO-I) Monoamine oxidase is an enzyme that breaks down dopamine. The MAO-I enables the body's naturally occurring dopamine to last longer.

The rasagiline helps my symptoms, and I have no nausea. But the instructions say to avoid tyramine-rich foods. Tyramine is an amino acid that helps regulate blood pressure. If you're on a MAO-I, tyramine could build up and cause elevated blood pressure levels. Foods with tyramine include draft beer, red wine, aged cheeses, tofu, and avocado—foods I eat all the time. Dr. Satinsky says the food issue isn't that important, but there it is, in writing on the medication package insert, and I'm uncomfortable ignoring it.

Since rasagiline could harm the liver, Dr. Andrew, my primary care doctor, orders liver function tests. Mine come back elevated. She says to stop the rasagiline; my LFTs go back to normal.

So Dr. Satinsky tries me on a different MAO-I called selegiline

(Eldepryl); I don't have to be so careful about tyramine in food with this medicine because it has more selective targets than the rasagiline. But it doesn't help as much as the rasagiline did.

The doctor says to add small doses of Sinemet, so I try half a tablet two times a day; I feel just awful, nauseous like the last time I tried it.

On the MAO-I, my symptoms are better, but they still bother me. I read more about Parkinson's medications, bring my notes to my next neurology appointment, and ask about other options.

Now Dr. Satinsky adds Mirapex, a dopamine agonist, which means that it mimics or boosts the effects of naturally occurring dopamine. Compared to being on no medication, my tremor is nearly gone, the rigidity is much better, and my hand coordination is improved. I think this might be the right regimen for me—selegiline and Mirapex together.

I like the way Dr. Satinsky works with me to find the best medication regimen, as each person is different. He's practicing "patient-centered care," which should be the model for all doctors. He tells me we should be able to eliminate my symptoms—wouldn't that be nice!

The medications I'm taking have different mechanisms of action. This approach of combining drugs with varying mechanisms of action, adding one at a time until you get a clinical response, is the same approach that was used to treat blood pressure in the Hypertension and Detection Followup Program study, where they call it stepped care. We used a similar approach to manage blood sugar levels in people with diabetes in a study that I worked on.

About a month later, my symptoms aren't entirely gone, so the doctor adds Amantadine—it's an anti-flu medication, but it helps Parkinson's symptoms, though they don't know how. About a week after I start the Amantadine, I'm walking around our apartment wearing shorts (it's summertime), and Bruce asks me, "What's wrong with your legs?"

"Nothing's wrong with my legs—they seem fine to me," I reply. "I've always thought I had pretty good legs."

"Well you do," he says, smiling. "But now they're all splotchy."

I look in a mirror. I have mottled gray splotches all over my thighs.

"Ew. What the heck? They look weird!"

I search for "splotchy legs in Parkinson's" online, and Amantadine comes up, right at the top. They actually use the word "splotchy" in the list of side effects. I call my doctor and tell him aout my legs. He says to gradually reduce and stop the Amantadine. Later he adds a Mirapex dose later in the day.

It takes five months to find an effective medication regimen for me because I have to try each medication for a couple of weeks before knowing how well it works.

So now I'm taking Sinemet, additional carbidopa (which reduces the nausea!), selegiline, Mirapex, and, for tremor and nerves, Klonopin. This 5-drug regimen works pretty well to reduce my symptoms, I'm getting some sleep, and am not so much on edge. The doctor says to gradually reduce the Klonopin because it makes me drowsy, and you're not supposed to take it for a long time.

It's hard to remember to take medicine once a day, let alone several times a day. To make it more complicated, some of my meds are taken twice and others three times a day.

During my clinical training, I would write out schedules for patients to make it easier for them: which pills to take in the morning, which mid-day, which in the evening. So I write out my own schedule. Every day I have to look at it; I can't seem to remember.

I take my mid-day pills to work in a little vial. One day at work, I can't find the vial, and my arm is getting stiff and trembling. I can't get through the day without my medicine, so I go home, find the vial where I left it on the kitchen counter, and take the meds right away. Eventually, I get a pill container with the days of the week, which helps a lot. And I leave a medication supply at work.

Almost all my medication bottles read, "may cause dizziness" and "alcohol intensifies effect" and "may cause dry mouth." I have mild dizzy spells, so I have to be careful to stand up slowly. I have dry mouth pretty much all the time, so now I chew gum a lot. I only slowly drink one drink during an evening—to be social. I really shouldn't be drinking at all.

No wonder a lot of patients with chronic disease don't take their medications correctly. It's not easy—even for someone with a medical degree.

Medical research is uncovering genetic associations and biological processes for Parkinson's, but it takes years—maybe decades—to develop new and better drugs. Drug companies spend massive amounts of money on research, much of which leads to blind alleys.

Three phases of research are required to get a drug approved: Phase 1 tests a drug's safety, phase 2 looks at its effects on biomarkers like chemical measurements in blood, and phase 3 trials test effects on patient clinical outcomes. After drug approval, sometimes strategy trials (called phase 4 trials by some) compare effects on clinical outcomes of different ways to use one or multiple drugs. For instance, I worked on a strategy trial about diabetes for ten years —ten years for just one study, the ACCORD study. More on ACCORD later.

I look up Parkinson's studies in progress, and I find a lot of basic science studies that are examining biological mechanisms and genetics; many of those studies are conducted using laboratory animals. Hopefully, these studies will identify mechanisms that can be exploited to develop new and better Parkinson's medications. Drug companies are examining different formulations of how to deliver dopamine—from infusions into the gut, to sublingual dopamine agonists. There are new medications on the horizon, such as a quick-acting drug to reduce "off" time—which is when the regular medication wears off, or symptoms return even when the medicine has been taken.

At least we have effective medications for Parkinson's symptoms.

My father had no medicines that could treat his ALS, a neurological condition that steals the ability to walk and later the ability to feed oneself, to swallow, and to breathe. There is only one approved medication for ALS, called riluzole. Based on clinical trials, the drug has a small effect on symptoms and increases survival by an average of only two months.

My dad testified at an FDA hearing in favor of their approval of riluzole. But he never got a chance to try it. One year after his diagnosis, he was gone.

PART 7: NIH STUDIES

*"The great tragedy of Science:
The slaying of a beautiful
hypothesis by an ugly fact."*

—Thomas Henry Huxley

Scratched Wood

I flipped on the light switch in the small, windowless office. A black desk chair sat at a small plain desk of medium-brown wood with a few scratches across its top. A maroon visitor's chair with a small rip in the seat upholstery sat behind the desk. A narrow wooden bookcase was bare except for one statistics book and one epidemiology book lying on their sides. I opened the metal file cabinet and saw a few files left behind by the previous occupant. The phrase "good enough for government work" came to mind.

It was 1992, and my new job was in the federal government's National Institutes of Health (NIH), the premier medical research center in the world. My position was in a branch, which was in a division, which was part of the National Heart, Lung, and Blood Institute (NHLBI)—one of 27 institutes and centers that make up NIH. NIH is in the Department of Health and Human Services in the Executive Branch of the U.S. Federal Government, funded by our income taxes. Bill Clinton, the President of the United States, was now my boss—well, he was my boss's, boss's, boss's, boss's, boss's, boss's, boss. (seven bosses.)

It was hard to choose between two job offers: one from NIH and another from the University of Maryland medical school in Baltimore, my alma mater where I had taught epidemiology to medical students with Dr. Sherwin and from which I was given a dataset for my dissertation. Taking a job there would feel like going home. In contrast, I didn't know what to expect from working in the government.

Bruce had accepted a job at NIH, so we tried to figure out where to live if I worked at the medical school in Baltimore, and he worked at NIH in Bethesda—longer than an hour's drive apart on days when the traffic was good. If we lived halfway between the two places, I would worry about being far from our children's school. If we lived near NIH, I would have to commute to Baltimore, and I hate driving. Both of us working at NIH solved the problem—we could live near NIH.

When I went for the job interview at NIH, I met Jeff, the Branch chief who would be my supervisor. He, curly-haired and bearded, and I, with big Texas hair and large 1980's glasses, shook hands and sat down in his office. Stacks of papers filled every surface—desk, table, and floor. Later I found out that his office always looked like he was in the middle of reading a thousand papers—which he probably was. Jeff was wearing khakis and a comfortable sweater. I was in a navy blue "interview suit" of jacket and skirt, a white blouse, hose, and heels. Though seemingly dressed for different occasions, I immediately felt a connection.

Jeff explained to me that the job was in extramural NIH, which funds investigators across the nation to do research, as opposed to intramural NIH, where research is done at NIH laboratories or in the NIH clinical center. "But our extramural division is different than most," he told me, "Because we're actively involved in the science. At least for the multi-center studies," which is when multiple sites across the country conduct the same study and combine the data.

During my interview day, I met physicians, nutritionists, health educators, and behavioral scientists who were in the extramural program at NHLBI. Using transparencies and an overhead projector, I gave a presentation about the meta-analysis of studies testing approaches to improve health behaviors—the project I had worked on with Pat during my post-doctoral fellowship. They seemed interested; several people in the branch worked on health behaviors, and they were all interested in prevention.

At the end of a full day of meetings, I went back to Jeff's office to discuss how things went. I found out that I would not be the only physician in the group, like I was at the University of Texas. And I wouldn't be responsible for overseeing clinical care either, like I was at Baylor. I would work on clinical research.

Jeff handed me a large envelope. Dark orange color, with lines to write the addressee's name and mail stop, tied closed with a string—a government-issue interoffice envelope. I saw through the holes that it contained paper. "What's this?" I asked.

"I have your CV, so here's mine," he said. "You should know as much about me as I know about you."

A supervisor had never before given me his or her curriculum vitae. Visiting the restroom before I left, I peeked in the envelope. His education and training were pretty much the same as mine, but a decade earlier. So I would be working for a physician with interests similar to mine who had an amazing amount of experience.

Many famous landmark studies originated at NIH—studies that changed the face of medical care in the nation. One example is the Hypertension and Detection Followup Program, which showed that treating "mild hypertension" can reduce strokes (and that resulted in me treating a young grandmother for mild high blood pressure before doing so was accepted practice). Another example is the Lipid Research Clinics—Coronary Primary Prevention Study, which provided the first experimental evidence that lowering blood cholesterol reduces heart attack risk (and was a study that Dr. Sherwin and I had taught to medical students). I would work on prevention studies like these—randomized trials—the study design that provides the highest evidence of causality (as I had learned from the famous paper by A.B. Hill and from Dr. Sherwin).

Jeff walked me to the front door of the building. I had come from Texas, so I had no coat. It was cold outside. *I guess I'll need to buy a coat,* I thought.

I thought I'd be at NIH for maybe five years and then go back to academia. But NIH became my career home for two decades. I followed in Jeff's footsteps and learned a lot from him: how to do multi-center randomized trials, to insist on quality, to base everything on evidence as much as possible, to use a multidisciplinary study team. At one point, he said to me, "I need to get out of your way," meaning I couldn't move up into his position if he was still in it.

At Jeff's retirement party, 15 years after I came to work with him, I gave a PowerPoint presentation about his life (yes, PowerPoint at last). I scanned in photographs, graciously lent to me by his wife. The title of my talk— "Jeff ... This is Your Life"—showed brightly in red letters on a yellow background. "And Mine also?" faded in at the bottom.

I said that Jeff and I were alike. We both were psychology majors in college; we both went to state medical schools; we both went to public health schools that started with the letter H (Hopkins, Harvard). Jeff was the branch chief, and then I was the branch chief. Jeff was the director of a program of three branches, and then I was the director of the program. Jeff led a huge blood pressure trial, and then I led a huge diabetes trial. Jeff became "senior scientific advisor;" I did too.

Wait, there's more: We both had six letters in our last names. If you assign 1 for A, 2 for B, etc., add them up, and then add the resulting digits together—they both add to 10. And lastly, Jeff is interested in the effects of salt on blood pressure—my married name is Morton, like the salt.

A Pattern, Not A Diet

I was standing in the hallway behind Eva—a tall, thin nutritionist with curly hair—as she poked her head into Jeff's office. "Are you ready to meet with us?" she asked him. "Sure," Jeff replied. "Come on in."

Eva and I entered his office, moved stacks of paper off his table and chairs, put them on the floor, and sat down at his small round meeting table.

It was 1993, and we were there to discuss the start-up of a new randomized trial that would test the effects of different dietary patterns on blood pressure. "I'd like your help on how to set up the dietary pattern study," Eva said.

Our roles as NIH project officers included both administration and science, and I was invited to this meeting to learn more about the administrative processes—how you set up and oversee a multi-center study.

About 70 million adults in the U.S. have high blood pressure, also called hypertension—a condition that increases the risk of strokes, heart attacks, kidney disease, and death. By testing the effects of different diets on blood pressure, results of this study would have immediate implications for public health recommendations.

After approval within the National, Heart, Lung, and Blood Institute (NHLBI, our institute), Eva and Jeff had written and released a Request for Applications (RFA) that described the study's purpose: to conduct a feeding study (participants would be given all their food) that would test the effects on blood pressure of different dietary patterns. A peer-review group convened by NIH evaluated the applications.

Five clinical sites and one coordinating center were funded by cooperative agreements, meaning they needed to work together and with NHLBI staff on the research effort. A principal investigator (PI) headed each site.

"I know a lot about diet," Eva said to Jeff. "But I'll need input on other things, like blood pressure and statistics. And administrative issues."

"You'll have a multidisciplinary team," Jeff said. "Use your team. I'll be on it and so will Denise, so you'll have two physicians. You also have a statistician and another nutritionist. I can help with the administrative aspects."

"Great. So the steering committee of the study will be the PIs from each site plus me? And each member will have one vote?"

"Yes, that's pretty standard."

"The NHLBI only gets one vote?" I asked. "But isn't NHLBI in charge?"

"Well," Jeff said, "We're responsible for making sure the funding is well used—to assure a high-quality study. But when it comes to scientific decision-making, we play an equal role with the sites and coordinating center."

Looking at paper she had brought with her, Eva said, "I made a list of possible committees: measurement, intervention—maybe that should be 'diets'—statistics, publications."

"Statistics need to be considered in context," Jeff said. "You'll need content people along with the statisticians. So maybe instead of a statistics committee, it should be a design and analysis committee. I can be on the D&A committee."

"Thanks. That makes sense. We'll need a written charge for each committee."

"I'll give you the charges for similar committees from other studies," Jeff said. NHLBI had been sponsoring multi-center studies for decades, and past infrastructures and processes were handed down for use in new studies. "You can edit them to fit this study."

"Great. Can you help me figure out who should chair which committee?"

"I like to have each PI chair a committee. They can report on their committee deliberations on steering committee calls and meetings."

Each study committee would include members from all six research sites plus our NHLBI team. Eva would chair regular meetings of our team to discuss issues that arose or to plan the next steps.

About 25 people—investigators from the five sites, the coordinating center, and NHLBI—were sitting at a large table in a hotel conference room for the first meeting of the study.

After introductions, Jeff made a little speech: "You're starting a difficult task," he said. "You each designed a study on the same topic, but those designs aren't identical. So now you have to design a single study everybody will do. It's an intense experience, as some of you know. For others, it's the first time."

It was the first time for me.

"So let's get started. I understand Frank is on the agenda to present background information about prior studies," Jeff said.

Sporting a dark curly beard but no mustache and wearing round wire-rimmed glasses, Frank, one of the PIs and an expert on cardiovascular disease prevention, got up, walked to the front of the conference room, placed a stack of overheads next to the projector, and proceeded to put them on the projector, one by one, and explain them. (It was the early 1990s, and we were just on the cusp of getting PowerPoint.) He spoke in a soft voice; I had to cup my ear to hear him.

"Several studies, listed here, found that vegetarians have lower blood pressure than non-vegetarians." He switched to another overhead. "These studies found that people who eat a lot of fruits and vegetables, even if they aren't vegetarians, have lower blood pressure." And another overhead, "and these studies found that people who eat a lot of dairy products have lower blood pressure than others."

They were all observational studies—some case-control but mostly cohort studies (research designs introduced earlier). These studies were not definitive because, although they had controlled statistically for other exposures related to BP and to diet (called confounders), the researchers may not have known about all the confounders, let alone measured them—a typical situation for an observational epidemiologic study.

"Fruits and vegetables have a lot of potassium," Frank continued. "Dairy products have a lot of calcium. Could the effects on blood pressure be due to those micronutrients?" He put up another overhead. "These randomized trials asked that question. They tested the effects of potassium or calcium dietary supplements compared to a placebo. None of the studies found the hypothesized effect on blood pressure. So it may be that foods—perhaps entire dietary patterns—are important, rather than individual nutrients."

And that was why we were going to conduct a randomized trial to determine the effects of dietary patterns on blood pressure. A randomized trial controls for multiple confounders (both known and unknown) by randomly assigning participants to an intervention or control group. The groups differ, on average, only in the exposure of interest, which, in this case, would be the dietary pattern.

"We wrote in the RFA that we want to detect a blood pressure difference between diet groups of two millimeters," Jeff reminded the investigators. That's just one tick mark on the measuring device. "Is everybody thinking the same thing?" he asked.

Assuring that the study could detect a such a small difference was based on Sir Geoffrey Rose's premise that a small shift in a population distribution of a risk factor could have as much, or even greater, effect on population health than only treating high-risk individuals.

The lead statistician from the coordinating center nodded, "If we measure blood pressure multiple times at baseline and follow-up, it'll increase precision so we can detect a small effect."

"We already know weight loss can reduce high blood pressure in overweight people, and that salt affects blood pressure," Eva added. "So we should hold those constant."

"To hold weight constant, we'll need to give the participants the right number of calories, so they don't lose or gain weight," added one of the nutritionists.

After much discussion over multiple meetings, the investigators decided to compare the effects on blood pressure of three diets:

- A *"control diet"* similar to what a typical Americas were eating, with few fruits and vegetables, fairly high in fat, low in fiber and minerals.
- A *"fruits and vegetables diet"* high in fruits and vegetables (which are high in minerals like potassium and magnesium and in fiber), but otherwise similar to the control diet.
- A *"combination diet"* high in fruits and vegetables as well as in dairy products (high in potassium, magnesium, calcium, and fiber), and lower in total fat and saturated fat than the control diet.

About 500 adult participants would be recruited among the five field centers. BP below 120/80 was considered "normal" or "optimal;" BP above 160/95 required medications. So participants' BP needed to be between those two values (120/80 to160/95). These cut-points were based on definitions in existing clinical guidelines, sponsored by our Institute and widely followed in clinical practice.

Randomized participants were given all their food and were not supposed to eat anything else. They ate one meal a day at the clinical site and were given the rest of their food to take home. The three diets were referred to by code letters (A, B, C) to "blind" participants and staff as much as possible. This double blinding helps prevent bias in how participants are treated and how measurements are taken.

I was on the measurement committee, which had to decide which measurements would be taken and how to take them. This included measurements for participant eligibility, measurements during the feeding period, and outcome measurements at the end of the feeding period.

I attended the blood pressure measurement training, where the study sites were trained to use the same methods. In medical school, I had been taught to put a cuff on the patient's arm, inflate it to higher than you expect the BP to be, then listen with your stethoscope bell inside the patient's elbow to pulse sounds as you slowly let air out of the cuff. You first hear the the sounds at the systolic pressure; sounds disappear at the diastolic pressure.

In the study training, we were taught to have the patient sit quietly for five minutes with both feet on the ground, to choose a cuff the right size from several options, and to let the pressure out very slowly—one tick mark on the scale for each breath taken by the patient. The training took six hours—a lot longer than the five minutes of training I got in medical school. And so I learned the difference between the rigor of research methods compared with quicker methods used in clinical practice.

This type of trial—with highly controlled interventions (in this case, the diets), compliant participants, rigorous measurements, and high attendance—is called an efficacy study. Since participants were given all their food, results would not be muddied by questions about whether the participants actually ate what they were supposed to eat. Confounders would not cause differences in blood pressure between the diet groups because potential confounders would either be held constant (like weight and dietary sodium intake) or would be the same, on average, between the diet groups because of the randomization process (like sex, age, and race).

Five years later, I was sitting at my computer going through emails when Eva appeared in my doorway holding a thick binder filled with paper. "Do you have a few minutes?" she asked me. I was now her supervisor. "I just got results from the coordinating center. I want to show you something."

She entered my office, placed the binder on my desk, and opened it to a dog-eared page. "Look at this," she said, pointing to values in the binder. "Here are average blood pressure values at baseline for each diet group, and over here are values after eight weeks on their diets."

"Systolic pressure was six mm lower on the combination than the control diet?" I asked.

"Yeah. And look at the subgroup with hypertension. 11 millimeters!"

I looked up at her, wide-eyed. "Wow. That's as much as medication!"

It was astounding—a much greater effect than we had expected. So we now knew that the effects of diet on blood pressure were substantial—very clinically relevant, much larger than the two mm of mercury that the study was designed to detect.

The prestigious *New England Journal of Medicine* published the remarkable results in 1997. Since the combination diet was such a success, our institute proceeded to make it widely known as the DASH diet—named for the study, Dietary Approaches to Stop Hypertension. Details were (and still are) posted on the NHLBI website, including recipes.

The DASH dietary pattern includes a lot of fruits and vegetables (9 to 12 servings a day, depending on number of calories), low-fat dairy products (3 servings a day), whole grains, fish, poultry, beans, seeds, nuts, and vegetable oils. It's low in sweets and red meats, as well as in saturated and trans fats. The fruits, vegetables, and whole grains make it high in potassium, calcium, magnesium, and fiber.

Even as a vegetarian, I found it hard to eat the DASH diet. Every time you eat, three meals a day plus a snack, you need to eat two servings of fruits and/or vegetables. Rice, beans, pasta, cereal, and bread do not count as vegetables, nor, of course, as fruit!

A follow-up study using the same basic methods, called DASH-Sodium, found that the DASH diet reduced BP at each of three levels of sodium and that the lower the sodium, the lower the BP. The highest sodium level used was about what U.S. adults were eating at the time (3,400 mg per day), the middle level was roughly the recommended maximum (2,400 mg per day), and the lowest level was about 1,500 mg per day. *The New England Journal of Medicine* published the results in 2001.

Subsequent studies showed that only partially eating the DASH diet can help lower elevated BP. The diet can also im-prove elevated blood cholesterol.

At the time of this writing, the *U.S. News and World Report* has judged, several years in a row, that the DASH dietary pattern at the lowest sodium is the best diet for our health. With a reduc-tion in calories, it's also effective for weight loss. [Note: they judged the Mediterranean diet also to be good for our health; the two diets are similar in many respects.]

In addition to the primary analyses, the investigators conducted ancillary analyses. And so I was part of a group that looked at effects of the DASH diet compared to the control diet in participants categorized by angiotensinogen genotype. Angiotensinogen is a chemical involved in regulating blood pressure.

We found that DASH participants who had the genotype associated with greater risk of developing hypertension had more BP lowering from the DASH diet than other angiotensino-gen genetic groups! In other words, there was an interaction between genotype and dietary efficacy. (Remember the interaction talk I gave in Dr. Anneger's class?) Stated another way, angiotensinogen genotype modified the effect of the diet on blood pressure.

I had thought that genetics determined health parameters. In this case, however, genetics seemed instead to affect sensitivity to diet. That was a new way to think about genetics for me. It was premature to suggest moving this preliminary information into clinical practice, but it was intriguing and pointed in a direction for more research. Imagine in the future, when we have enough evidence, a physician telling his/her patients what diet will be best for their health based on their genetic makeup.

Together costing only about $15 million, the two DASH studies were a fabulous investment of our tax dollars. They provided strong evidence about healthy diets, demonstrated that blood pressure is quite sensitive to diet, showed that genes may modify sensitivity to diet, and provided a proven lifestyle strategy for lowering cardiovascular risk factors.

The DASH-sodium results later fed into a controversy about how much dietary sodium should be recommended to the public. We do these studies to inform practice, but what the scientific results actually mean for practice requires subjective interpretation, which, as we shall see later, can be controversial.

That said, we shouldn't wait to take action until we know everything—because we never will.

A Dull Ache In The Chest

"You can't combine different interventions in one statistical analysis," said the man standing next to an overhead projector at the front of the conference room. He wore glasses, a gray wool jacket with leather patches on the elbows, and a maroon silk tie. "All the intervention communities need to receive the exact same intervention."

I leaned over and whispered to an NIH colleague sitting next to me in the audience, "Who is this guy?"

"Oh, that's Henry," she whispered. "The lead statistician from the coordinating center."

I was surprised at what Henry was saying. They hadn't said that in their grant application. I raised my hand. "Henry, we need to discuss this. If the intervention isn't tailored to a community's needs, it probably won't be successful. All communities are different."

Mary, a sweet and dedicated blonde nurse from our institute's office for educational programs, was coordinating a national program to encourage rapid care of patients with heart attack symptoms, called the National Heart Attack Alert Program.

"We know that when people come to an Emergency Room

with heart attack symptoms," Mary had told me, "they should be treated quickly, within 30 minutes. But many people don't come to the ER soon enough for treatment to work. It's a big problem."

Newly available drugs, called thrombolytics, could break up clots in coronary arteries that supply blood to the heart muscle causing a heart attack (or myocardial infarction, MI). A saying "Time is Muscle" referred to the fact that the longer the time between the start of symptoms and treatment, the more heart muscle dies—a finding from several studies on the topic.

To be effective, thrombolytics have to be given soon after symptoms start. But some people with symptoms were waiting hours or even days to seek care. Heart attack symptoms could be just a dull ache in the chest, so people may think they're having indigestion or stress or that it's nothing and will go away. Sometimes they realize they're having a problem, but they don't call an ambulance because they don't want neighbors to see or hear it, or they want someone they know to drive them. How do we know this? They told us …in focus groups.

So in 1994, we started a new study to determine whether a community-wide education program would improve patient care-seeking and reduce delay time—the time from onset of symptoms to arrival at an ER. We also wanted to find out if the program would result in more use of emergency services, like calling 911 for an ambulance, or alternatively whether it would result in overwhelming ERs with people who didn't need to be there.

Behavior as the primary outcome for a study is rare at NIH where outcomes examined in most clinical studies are clinical events, like a heart attack or death, or are blood measures or other biological tests. Since behaviors are so important to health, I was pleased that Jeff asked me to be the NHLBI lead on this study.

I wrote my first request for applications (RFA), and we got about 35 applications—a great response. We funded five field centers, each with four study communities, totaling twenty communities for the study as a whole. We also funded a coordinating center. The field centers, coordinating center, and our research office at NHLBI would all work together to design, implement, evaluate, and report the same multi-center study.

Communities, rather than individuals, would be randomly assigned to intervention or comparison groups because the intervention program would be directed at the entire community. Communities would be matched into pairs based on demographics. (For example, two largely Hispanic communities were matched, and two with a high percentage of African-Americans were matched.) After four months of baseline measurements of delay time, one community of each pair would be chosen by an electronic flip of the coin to receive the intervention program and the other to just have measurements taken.

Based on a naming contest amongst the researchers, we called the study REACT, for Rapid Early Action for Coronary Treatment. That is a great acronym because it indicated what we wanted people to do—react to their symptoms—and not only that, it's pronounceable!

I asked Mary from the educational office to be on the intervention committee, and she and I set up a great working relationship between the research branch I was in and the educational office she was in.

A large man blocked my office doorway, filling it, his head grazing the top of the opening. I looked up. "A little birdie told me you wanna talk about study design and analysis," he said. It was Mike P, the statistician on our NHLBI team for the REACT trial.

Mike P was a sweetheart, and he was funny and kind. Over the years he taught me a lot about statistics, including the concept that real data are immensely better than estimating missing data (so it's better just not to have any missing data!), and that statistical modeling is always based on assumptions that may not be true.

"Yeah, thanks for coming, Mike," I said. "Have a seat."

He sat down in my guest chair—the one with the ripped upholstery.

"What do you think of Henry's statement that all the communities need to get the exact same intervention?"

"Well, that's how they do randomized trials of drugs. All the patients get the same drug or a placebo," he said. "But this is different. This is in the real world, not a laboratory."

That made sense. Mike always made sense.

"Is there a way we could tailor interventions to the different communities and still combine the results into one analysis?"

We discussed the issue a while. Then the intervention and the design and analysis committees discussed it. Later at a Steering Committee meeting, Russell, the study chair, said, "Committees have discussed the issue Henry brought up at the first meeting. Do the interventions need to be identical? I understand we have a proposal."

The proposal was to test a strategy of intervention—an intervention program, with multiple components. Every intervention community would get a program to educate patients, their families, clinicians, and the entire community about the importance of seeking care for heart attack symptoms. They would all get the same core messages: what symptoms to look for (chest pain or discomfort along with other symptoms such as shortness of breath, sweating, nausea, or weakness) and actions to take (call 911 if symptoms persist for 15 minutes or longer). A two-phase analysis would be conducted. First, the slope of delay time over calendar time in each community would be determined, and then the slopes in intervention communities would be compared to slopes in control communities.

Most prior intervention studies in community settings (such as schools, worksites, or entire communities) had targeted many behaviors at once (i.e., diet, smoking, and exercise) and were only modestly, if at all, successful. Intervention studies in individuals had been more successful when they used multiple avenues to target changes in one specific behavior. Now we were going to test that approach in entire communities.

We thought, but didn't know, that the intervention program would work. If we already knew it would work, it would not have been ethical to have a control group.

What happened? Well, the intervention program did NOT reduce delay time. It did, however, increase ambulance use by people with chest pain—one of several secondary outcomes that we wanted to happen. And it didn't overwhelm the ERs.

Despite disappointing results on the primary outcome, because the REACT study was large, well conducted, and important, the *Journal of the American Medical Association* published the findings in 2000. Our institute's press release bore this title: *"Education Study Increases Ambulance Use but Yields No Extra Improvement in Heart Attack Patient Delay Time."* Though the press release noted that the intervention increased ambulance use, that was only one of several secondary outcomes. There was a pretty high likelihood that the result came out significant just by chance alone—not because it was real. (You may remember the issue of multiple comparisons we discussed earlier.) Readers of the published paper should at least be told what the prespecified primary outcome was, which the REACT paper did. (It was delay time.)

We learned a lot from REACT. For one thing, we probably need more intensive and lengthy interventions in tackling a community problem. The 18-month intervention period wasn't long enough to build support, a following, momentum, community partnerships, community action. Surveys of community residents showed there wasn't much recognition of the messages. And there was no attempt to change the system— for example, by administering thrombolytics in ambulances —which might have been more effective than community education.

Although the results of REACT were a bit disappointing, our institute proceeded to convert the intervention materials and messages into a format for use across the nation, with some modifications based on the REACT experience. These materials became part of the National Heart Attack Alert Program.

So the institute was following the principle that we need to use whatever evidence we do have, even if it's incomplete, rather than do nothing. Several years later, new Institute leadership discontinued the National Heart Attack Alert Program, although some of their educational materials are still available online. Mary took a job elsewhere in government. (But I later hired her back.)

I started working on REACT about five years after I was Dr. Annegers' teaching assistant. I learned a huge amount from him, and every day I used what I learned. But I don't remember ever telling him that we were trying to get people to seek medical care right away when they have heart attack symptoms, which could be just a dull ache in the chest.

One Saturday in 2000, he was found dead in the bathroom at the School of Public Health where he taught in Houston, Texas. He was 55 years old. I heard he had been complaining of some chest discomfort. He had ridden his bike to work.

I so much regret not telling him about the messages of REACT. It may not have made a difference, but maybe it could have saved his life.

Counseling In Practice

Our entire division of about 60 people filled a large conference room for our 1993 "winter review." Our division director, branch chiefs, and staff who had an item on the agenda sat at the huge conference table. Other staff sat in chairs in the periphery—the "peanut gallery."

Claude Lenfant, our institute director, chaired the meeting. Our institute director for 25 years, Claude ran our institute with an imposing autocratic flair. Tall and fit, looking younger than his age, and with a strong French accent, we (his staff) thought *"L'etat, c'est moi,"* ("the state, it is me") must have been his motto. Though we sometimes thought he managed by intimidation, we always knew where he stood. Even if he disapproved a request, which happened often, it was far better than waiting a long time to hear, which happened more after he left.

This meeting was not a venue for general discussion; it was a venue to present proposals to Claude. The only people to speak were those on the agenda, or those Claude spoke to directly. The purpose was to present proposed initiatives—institute-initiated research programs—for possible funding. These are studies in response to NIH requests, such as RFAs or other funding opportunity announcements. These institute initiatives comprised about 25% of NIH extramural funding; the remaining 75% of extramural funding was for investigator-initiated studies not in response to any NIH funding announcement. An initiative could be for multiple studies in a topic area or a single multi-center study. Staff writeups included a science summary, rationale for the initiative, key research questions, type and number of studies to be funded, number of years, and amount of funding requested.

For this particular meeting, I was on the agenda to propose an initiative for a new multi-center study about physical activity—the first initiative I originated. "This study would test education and counseling approaches designed to increase physical activity in sedentary outpatients," I told Dr. Lenfant. "Programs would be practical for delivery in primary care doctors' offices. New programs would be compared to usual care."

Claude looked up at me from his briefing book. "Hmmm... Why is this important?"

That was the first time he had spoken to me directly. Much later we would speak occasionally at one-on-one meetings in his office after hours, talking about things like whether extramural staff should write scientific papers (I thought we should, if we were scientifically involved in the studies) and how to budget large studies (I thought budgets should be realistic, not trimmed to get approval). He told me once that my views were too narrow, that I should think about the bigger picture, rather than only my group's activities. That was good advice—advice I did try to follow, especially later when I had a higher position. But right now, I was focused on this one initiative proposal.

I said, "Well, we know that physical activity is important for health." Findings from research on physical activity and cardiovascular disease met nearly all of Hill's evidence of causality. "Doctors are supposed to advise their patients to exercise. But doctors usually aren't trained in health behavior change or exercise methods, so they're often not sure how to do it." I looked at him to see his reaction—criticizing doctors maybe wasn't a good idea.

"Hmmm... yes, that seems right," he said.

So I continued, "We need research to test approaches that doctors and other healthcare providers could use in clinical practice. We need to test them in real clinical practice settings to see what approaches actually will work to help patients become more active."

I had chosen this topic because the meta-analysis I did with Pat during my fellowship had found very few randomized trials testing education or counseling approaches for physical activity in clinical settings. After coming to NIH, I had written a review of the relevant literature, had presented the concept to our program's advisory committee ("They're our friends," Jeff had said. "They're here to help us.") and had developed a budget estimate for the project based on Jeff's advice. ("Whatever budget amount you tell Claude," Jeff had told me, "is what he'll always remember for the project.") So I was prepared for the next question.

"How much would it cost?" Claude asked.

"About ten million over five years—two million a year," I said. It was expensive but within the range of a moderately-sized, five-year multi-center randomized trial at the time. He studied the numbers in the briefing book.

"Okay," he said. "It can go to Council," which was a high-level committee of national experts whose advice is required for the institute to release initiatives and fund grants.

A couple of months later, wearing my best (and only) suit, I stood at the podium in a large, well-appointed room in a building on the NIH campus. A huge oval table of polished wood with built-in microphones filled the center of the room. Deans, department chairmen, and professors from medical schools, some with named professorships (like "The Tom Walton Chair of Pediatrics"), sat in armchairs at the table along with our institute leadership—five division directors and Claude. Staff packed the chairs in the peanut gallery. I had just presented my proposed initiative to test interventions delivered in primary care to increase physical activity in sedentary patients and had asked for questions or comments.

Most Council members at that time, in 1993, were gray-haired, middle-aged white men who wore dark suits, often with white shirts and maroon ties. There were maybe two women and one minority out of a dozen or so Council members. Now one of the gray-haired, middle-aged men raised his hand, leaned forward, turned on his microphone, looked at me, and said, "It would be unethical to have usual care for a control group."

What? I thought, taken aback. Usual medical care isn't ethical? How could our nation's medical system be unethical? I had recently spent three years working in that system.

"Perhaps I wasn't clear," I replied. "The patients would get their regular medical care. The study wouldn't deny patients care they would normally get."

"But we know doctors don't advise patients to exercise, even though they should," he continued. "I can't approve this study unless all the patients get more than they normally would—even the patients in the control group."

I wanted to study what additional things doctors and their staff could do, over and above what they usually do, to help sedentary patients become active. The Council member wanted us to study what doctors and their staff could do over and above the current recommended standard of care. Those are two different objectives. Usual care (what is typically delivered) often doesn't meet current standards (what is recommended in guidelines or by expert bodies). Most clinical trials study the effects of medications or medical procedures, and I didn't know that control groups for those studies are usually the recommended standard of care—because the purpose of the study is to push the boundaries of the science. But this was a different type of research, an applied research study, uncommon at NIH, which would study approaches to implement what we already knew was important for health.

Claude asked me to work with the Council member until he was satisfied. So, to get the initiative approved, and with Jeff's input, I changed the research question. I changed the control group to be the current standard of care—physician advice.

We funded three clinical sites and a coordinating center for a multi-center study. Steve, the physical activity epidemiologist who had advised us on the handbook project in Texas, chaired the steering committee. Though I only had one vote on the five-person steering committee, I told them the study protocol had to have physician advice for the control group because that's what had been approved. In retrospect, I probably could have allowed them to change it (and they did want to change it—to usual care), but I didn't know that at the time.

And so we started the Activity Counseling Trial (ACT), which tested whether either or both of two educational programs would improve physical activity and fitness compared with physician advice. We asked this question separately in men and women. With three intervention groups, two sexes, and two outcomes, there would be multiple comparisons. If you remember Dr. Annegers' class, you would wonder whether we adjusted for multiple comparisons. Of course we did; our statisticians insisted on it—these were, after all, the primary outcomes for the study (unlike in REACT where ambulance use was a secondary outcome).

After two years of delivering the interventions, we saw the results. In the women, there was a small but significant increase in fitness in both intervention groups compared with physician advice. Some of the study investigators had thought the less intensive intervention wasn't even worth testing, but it had the same effect on fitness as the more intensive intervention. There were no effects on self-reported physical activity, however, so the results were inconsistent.

In the men, there was an increase in fitness compared with baseline in all three groups—but no difference comparing the groups. We had no idea whether the physician advice helped improve fitness, because there was no non-advice control group for comparison.

We published the results in *the Journal of the American Medical Association* in 2001. Our press office stressed the most positive finding by titling the press release: *"NHLBI Study Finds Brief Counseling By Health Professionals Boosts Patients' Physical Fitness."*

About 15 years later, the Center for Medicaid and Medicare Services (CMS) declared obesity to be a disease and said it would consider reimbursing medical care shown to be effective in reducing weight in obese patients. So I wrote a new initiative that would fund three randomized trials testing weight-loss interventions in real-world clinical practice settings—a similar concept to the ACT study, though focused on obesity, and three separate studies rather than one multi-center study.

The initiative sailed through the approval process, and we funded three randomized trials called POWER for Practice-based Opportunities for Weight Reduction. Weight-loss interventions in two of the trials significantly reduced weight in obese patients over two years compared with a minimal intervention control group given written materials. Similar to many weight-loss studies that had been conducted in research settings, the participants lost the greatest amount of weight over the first six months, and then they started to gradually gain much of the weight back over the remaining 18 months of intervention. Still, weight was lower at two years than at baseline.

Before the POWER studies, we didn't know whether weight-loss strategies would be effective if provided through a primary care office. They were. *The New England Journal of Medicine* published the results in 2005. Later, the influential US Preventive Services Task Force recommended that clinicians use "intensive, multicomponent behavioral interventions" for weight loss in obese patients.

We know how to help overweight people lose weight. First, motivation is crucial. Then setting realistic goals for amount of weight to lose as well as for diet and physical activity, aiming for a modest calorie deficit. Next, monitoring progress, like doing daily or weekly weighings and keeping exercise and/or food diaries. Usually problem solving is needed to figure out what, if anything is getting in the way of success. These steps have been proven to result in five to seven percent weight loss —an amount shown to improve, on average, cardiovascular risk factors like blood pressure and cholesterol. Once monitoring is discontinued, however, weight often goes back up.

Losing weight is not rocket science. But it is hard to do! There is incredible pressure from environmental, social, and cultural influences that make weight loss difficult, and keeping it off even more difficult.

Preventing weight gain in the first place may be easier for many people. But we don't seem to be giving that message. The average American adult gains one to two pounds a year (often around the winter holidays) and doesn't lose them. After twenty years, you can calculate how much weight gain that would be. (Hint: 20 to 40 pounds).

My personal experience in preventing weight gain comes from my use of a what I'm calling a Choices Diet. It's a very simple concept about being mindful about what you eat: Whenever you eat or drink anything, at any time, you need to make a choice about what to eat (or buy or cook). So the "diet" consists of choosing the healthiest and/or lowest-calorie option or a smaller portion size. In a nutshell, choose lots of vegetables and fruits, low-fat dairy, whole grains, not much animal fat (like the DASH or Mediterranean diets).

What shall I have for lunch today? A cheeseburger and fries, or some tomato soup and a small salad? What shall I drink with my lunch? Coke, diet coke, orange juice, water? It's your choice. (Hint: choose the soup and salad, and the water.)

Choose a target weight for yourself (which could be your current weight if you want to stop gaining), add regular weighings (at least weekly), and whenever your weight creeps up a pound or two, use the choices concept and be mindful about what you choose to eat. If you do this when you are just a pound or two over your goal, you never have to lose more than a few pounds, deprive yourself of foods you love, or worry about large weight swings, which are not good for you. This concept has not been tested directly, as far as I know, but takes into account information gleaned from multiple studies. Let me know if it works for you.

A Bit Of Sugar

Peter, our division director and a physician epidemiologist, visited us, his division staff, every morning in what some of us called his morning rounds—a holdover term from patient rounds during medical training. We joked that just walking around the hallways, he accumulated his goal of 10,000 steps a day.

Early one morning in 1999, Peter stopped at my office as I was hanging my coat on the hook on the back of my office door. "Do you have a minute?" he asked.

I was now a research group leader and in a larger office with some more attractive furniture that I had scrounged from unused surplus, including a small, round meeting table. I gestured to the table, and we both sat down. "What's up?" I asked.

Thin as a rail and with wavy blondish hair, Peter leaned forward, looked at me, and said, "I want you to be the project officer for ACCORD." He paused and then added, "Claude agrees."

ACCORD (Action to Control Cardiovascular Risk in Diabetes) was a large study about diabetes and cardiovascular disease that our institute recently had started. At the time, I was supervising the ACCORD project officer, a physician-researcher in the group I was leading.

"ACCORD needs someone with more experience," Peter said, which I now had because of studies I have described (DASH, DASH-Sodium, REACT, ACT) as well as others.

"I'm flattered you asked me. ACCORD is so important to the

institute."

"Being in charge of ACCORD will be good for your career."

Perhaps, but at nearly 50 years old, I wanted to supervise project officers, not be one myself. It seemed clear that Peter wasn't asking me—he was telling me. How could I say no?

In 1999 when we started ACCORD, a gallon of gas cost $1.22, Bill Clinton was impeached and acquitted, and we were all scared that our computers would blow up when the year 2000 was reached. All of these things came and went as I worked as the scientific project officer on ACCORD—one of the largest, longest, and most expensive trials ever supported by NIH.

Why would the Heart, Lung, and Blood Institute fund a study about diabetes? Because most people with diabetes have Type 2 diabetes (previously called adult-onset diabetes), and most people with Type 2 diabetes die of cardiovascular disease rather than of their diabetes. Perhaps the high blood sugar in diabetes (called *hyperglycemia*)—the diagnostic hallmark of diabetes—causes cardiovascular disease? If so, reducing the glycemia may reduce cardiovascular events such as heart attacks, strokes, and cardiac deaths. We also needed more evidence on how to treat blood pressure and blood lipids/cholesterol to reduce cardiovascular events in type 2 diabetes.

According to the CDC, an estimated 12 million people in the U.S. had diabetes at the time ACCORD started. So, the ACCORD results would inform how millions of people with diabetes would be treated in clinical practice! Furthermore, ACCORD results would be directly relevant to practice the day the results were released, because the study would use medications already approved and available for use in clinical care—but it would use them in a new strategy that focuses on glycemia targets.

There was a lot of evidence that diabetes was a risk factor for cardiovascular disease, and that it may actually be a cause.

Peter, my Division Director had, along with others, gathered much of that evidence.

Considering Hill's items for causality, in 1999 we knew that:

• Adults with type 2 diabetes had higher rates of cardio-vascular disease than adults without type 2 diabetes (association).

• Diabetes often occurred before cardiovascular disease (temporal sequence).

• The higher the glycemia, the higher the rate of cardiovascular disease in population groups (dose-response).

• Controlling for confounders, the associations persisted (specificity).

• Multiple studies had similar findings (consistency).

• High blood sugar can injury artery walls by several mechanisms identified through animal studies (biological plausibility).

But there was no experimental evidence in humans that lowering hyperglycemia would reduce cardiovascular events. Prior randomized trials examining the issue had either been stopped early because of harm, like the University Group Diabetes Trial (UGDP, published in 1960), or had inconclusive results on cardiovascular disease, like the United Kingdom Prospective Diabetes Study (UKPDS, published in 1998). UKPDS did, however, show benefit for small vessel diseases of the eyes and kidneys. An expert committee convened by our institute had recommended a new randomized trial to address how to treat hyperglycemia, blood pressure, and blood lipids to reduce cardiovascular disease.

When I took over as scientific project officer for ACCORD, I reorganized our NHLBI project team of research physicians, nurses, and statisticians, plus a contract officer for budgetary issues. I appointed a deputy project officer and assigned team members to the various study committees (e.g., recruitment, measurement, blood pressure, cholesterol, glycemia, publications) and as liaisons to parts of the infrastructure (coordinating center, seven clinical networks, a drug distribution center, and pharmaceutical companies that donated medications but otherwise had no input into the study). I chaired a weekly team meeting to discuss issues from study committees, monitor study progress, discuss and solve problems, and proactively plan.

I served as the lead NIH scientist on the ACCORD steering committee, along with the principal investigators of the seven clinical networks and the coordinating center. So, the steering committee comprised eight men, most of whom were middle-aged white men with beards, and me. The steering committee vice chair jokingly referred to us as Snow White and the eight dwarves. I wasn't offended; I actually thought it was a way I was being welcomed.

Bill, a terrific study chair, set the tone for decision-making. The nine-member steering committee would need written proposals in order to take a vote, a simple majority would allow a proposal to pass, and we wouldn't revisit an issue unless new information came to light. I had worked on other studies where people couldn't let go of a position—even after they lost a vote, they would continue to lobby and bring the issue up again and again. (Kind of like the Congressional Republicans and Obamacare, 2010-2018.) But in ACCORD, people accepted voting results and graciously moved on to work together.

Seventy-seven clinical centers across the U.S. and Canada would recruit about 10,000 participants with adult-onset type 2 diabetes. The participants had to be at high risk for a heart attack; about one third had preexisting cardiovascular disease. After providing informed consent, they would enter the glycemia trial and either the blood pressure or the lipid trial.

The coordinating center would randomly assign all the

participants to one of two glycemia strategies that targeted different A1C levels. A1C is a measure of average blood sugar over the prior three months and is used routinely in clinical practice to assess glucose control in people with diabetes. An intensive treatment strategy would treat A1C down to a level seen in non-diabetic adults (less than 6%). A standard treatment strategy would target A1C as typical for practice (about 7.5%). Both groups would be followed for several years to see if the intensive A1C group had lower rates of cardiovascular events (heart attacks, strokes, deaths) than the standard group.

The ACCORD blood pressure trial would test a strategy to lower blood pressure to the 'normal' range of less than 120 systolic compared with a standard treatment target of less than 140. The ACCORD lipid trial would test using a fibrate plus a statin to lower LDL cholesterol and triglycerides as well as to increase HDL, compared with only a statin to lower LDL.

Therefore, for all three ACCORD trials—glycemia, blood pressure, lipids—the control groups would be given the current standard of care. All the ACCORD participants would get as good, if not better, care then they would outside the study in their usual care setting.

After many five to four decisions by the steering committee (science planning is challenging) a study protocol was ready for review by a committee of outside experts invited by the NHLBI. Study investigators presented the proposed study design, and the protocol review committee asked questions and discussed issues. The committee was mainly concerned that the clinical sites wouldn't be able to reach the intensive treatment target, and to do so safely. So they recommended a vanguard phase of a thousand participants. If successful, a full-scale trial of 10,000 participants would be considered.

And so we commenced detailed planning and gearing up for a vanguard phase. Each of the 77 clinics, seven networks, and coordinating center got approvals from their Institutional Review Board for human subjects (IRB). The coordinating center designed and held a training meeting attended by 300 study staff. The ACCORD study was off and running!

Well, "off and running" was a pipe dream. One issue after another arose. IRBs wanted changes to the informed consent document. The drug distribution center didn't have enough drugs available yet for all the patients. The recruitment rate was too slow.

A new issue arose daily. So we adopted a motto: "ACCORD: It's always something." I considered getting buttons made.

After about a year and a half of the vanguard phase—solving issue after issue—I arrived at Claude's large corner office to brief him on the vanguard results. Sitting at his meeting table along with Peter and Jeff, I handed out a packet of information marked CONFIDENTIAL. The study reached the recruitment goal of a thousand patients within four months. The blood pressure levels were excellent, with a big difference between the standard and intensive groups, as we wanted. Adherence to the blinded medication in the lipid trial was very high, which was the goal. As for the glycemia trial, the average A1C in the intensive group was lower than in the standard group, as was desired, but not in the non-diabetic range as we wanted.

"So," Peter concluded, "they met all the vanguard goals except for glycemia, where they came close."

"The investigators are discussing tweaking the glycemia treatment protocol," I added.

"Tweak? What do you mean 'tweak'?" Claude asked.

"Well, a few small changes to make sure the glycemia difference between groups is bigger: like pushing glycemia down harder and sooner in the intensive group and waiting a tad longer in the standard group to see how well study medications are working. Just getting free medications seems to be reducing glycemia, even if it's the same regimen they were on before."

"So how much will it all cost?" he asked.

"Well..." I looked at Peter, then at Jeff, then at Claude. I swallowed hard. "Claude, we got draft budgets from all the sites for a full-scale trial of 10,000 participants. I'm sorry to say... but the vanguard made it clear it'll take a lot more effort than we thought—a lot more staff time. So it'll cost a lot more—three times as much as we originally thought—about 35 million dollars a year, for a total of about $350 million over the study duration." That amount was as much each year as a large multi-center trial would cost in its entirety over several years. That amount could fund about a hundred individual grant studies. [For comparison the Lockheed Martin/Boeing F-22 Raptor cost about $200 million per fighter in 2010, and the DOD budget included 188 of them. Just pause and think a moment about government funding priorities.]

Claude's face grew dark. "This is serious money." He frowned. "I will convene a special group of experts to review the findings and advise me on whether the study is worth the cost."

And so Claude invited a special advisory group, and we, the study group, waited to find out whether ACCORD would continue into the full-scale trial. While we were waiting, as a humorous aside, I made a fake movie called, of course, "ACCORD: the movie." I asked key people whom they wanted to play them. I presented it in PowerPoint to the group (yes, we did have PowerPoint by then):

"In this medical thriller, a renegade group of diabetologists goes on a quest to find better treatments to reduce heart attacks in people with diabetes. All is not well, however, when one issue after another needs to be resolved. With an all-star cast, Sean Connery plays Bill, the Steering Committee Chair [a photo of Sean Connery appears—he really looks just like Bill!]; Tom Cruise plays Hertzel who leads the glycemia committee [a photo of Tom Cruise appears], And Demi Moore plays Denise from the NIH project office [Demi Moore's photo appears—of course, I chose my own star]... Rated PG-13 for medical jargon and tense medical situations."

The audience loved it. (I still have the PowerPoint slides somewhere.)

Finally, Claude got the recommendation from the special committee: they said that ACCORD should go forward because it was asking critical questions for clinical practice. I had attended the committee's meeting, and I wasn't sure they grasped the broader financial context. But Claude approved ACCORD to continue into the full-scale trial, and he requested an extensive monitoring plan, which we developed and put into place.

By that time, the study had become important to me, and I had learned an enormous amount by working with the best investigators in the country. If I had taken the job in academia instead of at NIH, I never would have gotten the opportunity to work on something this big.

And so for ten years I spent half my time on ACCORD and became known within the institute for the study. It was stressful dealing with such a large enterprise for which there was "always something" that we needed to handle—it was a huge amount of work.

I got tired of institute staff, especially directors of other divisions, mentioning the expense of ACCORD and then glaring at me as if I had gotten us into it. They weren't happy that it used resources that could have funded a lot of smaller studies. When given the opportunity, I would point out that, although it was only one study, it was asking three important questions, and it supported more than a hundred investigators.

And that it wasn't my fault. (It was Peter's.)

Wait, What?

W ho's responsible for patient safety in a clinical trial? Well, everybody involved is. The study investigators and staff, the IRB at the investigator's institution, the Data and Safety Monitoring Board (DSMB) appointed by NIH, the NIH funding institute. When do you decide a safety issue warrants a change, like stopping a study or making protocol changes? The answers are a matter of judgment. It depends on whether the data are convincing, for example, whether there is statistical significance. It depends on how important the measurement is, for example, whether it's death or a minor abnormality in a blood value. Someone's opinion may depend on whether they are considered legally liable. Entire books have been written on this difficult subject.

One calm day in 2007, when I was sitting at my computer, going through emails, my phone rang. Looking at the caller ID, I picked up the receiver and said, "Hi Bob, what's up?" Bob was the principal investigator of the ACCORD coordinating center, which conducted the analyses and developed interim data reports for monitoring.

"I'm going through the draft data report for the upcoming DSMB meeting," he said. "It looks like we might have an issue in the glycemia trial." At that time, we NIH staff could see monitoring data, but investigators and staff in the clinical sites could not. Later NIH would change the policy so the project office staff couldn't see monitoring data because of potential conflicts of interest. But I was glad I could see the data because I don't know how I could have been ready for what was about to happen if I didn't know what was coming. But I'm getting ahead of the story...

"An issue?" I asked.

"There's a slightly higher death rate—total mortality—in the intensive glycemia group than in the standard group."

"A higher death rate? In the intensive group? Really?" I paused. "Do you think it's real?"

"It's small and not significant. It could be a fluke, a statistical fluctuation—there's not much follow-up time yet and not many events. But it could be a signal." A signal that the intensive glycemia treatment is harmful—contrary to the study hypothesis that it would be beneficial.

"Did you double check the data coding?" I had to ask.

"Of course, triple checked!"

Because this was an early look and not much data, the difference in mortality rates that Bob noticed could have gone away over time as more data were collected.

Preparing for the next DSMB meeting several months later, I reviewed a new draft data report. The higher mortality in the intensive glycemia compared with the standard glycemia group not only had continued but now was borderline significant, with a p-value exactly at 0.05 (a p-value less than 0.05 is generally considered significant).

If the analyses had been statistically adjusted for multiple looks over time, to adjust for multiple comparisons, it would not have been significant. So I wasn't convinced the finding was robust enough for the DSMB to recommend changes. The difference could have been due to chance and not real.

The DSMB spent a long time in executive session at their meeting. The intensive glycemia strategy had not reduced cardiovascular rates as hypothesized. At the same time, the strategy seemed to increase the risk of dying. These were completely unexpected results.

So the DSMB provided a strong recommendation to stop the

intensive glycemia treatment because of harm. The institute director, now Betsy (Claude had retired), accepted the recommendation.

After the DSMB meeting, Yves, a clinical trialist and my deputy project officer for ACCORD at the time, and I discussed the situation. "We have to stop the intensive glycemia treatment," I said, "but they made no recommendation about the blood pressure and lipid trials. Maybe we could transfer the intensive glycemia patients into the standard glycemia strategy and continue the blood pressure and lipid trials."

"Yeah, we probably could do that," Yves said, "since all the participants are in either the blood pressure or lipid trial, in addition to being in the glycemia trial."

"We need to discuss this with our team and the coordinating center. And I'll need to run it by Betsy."

"It'll be a huge amount of work to stop the intensive glycemia," Yves said. "We'll need to inform the investigators, the patients, the study staff."

"Yeah. We'll need to tell the steering committee in confidence, so they can help us plan. We don't want a leak before we have a clear message. And we'll have to decide whether to announce it before we publish a scientific paper."

"I'll take out our contingency closeout plans and share them with the coordinating center." We had been working in secret on plans for several months, just in case.

Betsy approved the plan to transition all the intensive glycemia participants to the standard glycemia treatment and finish up the blood pressure and lipid trials. She also decided we should release the main findings before a paper could be published because of the importance and surprising finding that the intensive treatment increased death rates.

Yves worked with the coordinating center on logistics and messages to the patients, investigators, and study staff. I wrote, and then answered, Questions and Answers for the NHLBI website , which are still online. Our press officer drafted a press release, also online. We each reviewed each other's work and sent back and forth comments and edits. I could barely keep up. (At least my kids were off at college, so I had a lot of time I could work.)

Finally, after a couple of weeks, everything was done. We held a special mandatory teleconference with the steering committee investigators and told them about the changes. We decided they would inform their patients and start transferring them to the standard strategy the same day NHLBI released a press release and held a telephone press conference. The press release title read: *A Therapeutic Strategy Targeting Blood Sugar to Near-Normal Levels Does Not Reduce Cardiovascular Events but Increases Mortality in Persons with Diabetes at High Risk*. Though pretty long, an accurate title.

We gathered for the press conference in a conference room on the NIH campus down the hall from Betsy's office—Betsy, Peter, the press officer, our new division director (Mike L), and me. Key study investigators and the Steering Committee chair were on the phone. About five minutes before the press conference was to start, Betsy's assistant entered the conference room and whispered in Betsy's ear. She got up and walked out of the room.

"What's going on?" I asked. "Why is she leaving so close to the press conference?"

"She's going to take a telephone call," her assistant said.

We all looked at each other, wondering what was going on, waiting for her to return. Who was she talking to on the phone, and why now?

Ten minutes after she left, she returned. "I talked to the president of the American Diabetes Association. I want to make sure our messages are consistent, so we don't confuse the public."

I understood why she wanted to inform the ADA. But it could take months, maybe years, to really understand what the findings meant and to combine this new information with other research evidence to inform practice.

Two other large randomized trials on the same topic (called ADVANCE and VA-DT) presented their findings at the same meeting we presented ACCORD's—the 2008 American Diabetes Association meeting, a huge annual scientific meeting with about 20,000 attendees. None of the three trials had found that intensive glycemia treatment reduced cardiovascular events. Only ACCORD reported increased mortality rates.

What caused the higher mortality rates in ACCORD? Speculation was rampant. Some said it was a too rapid lowering of glycemia. Others said it must have been the increase in hypoglycemia (blood sugar too low). Yet others thought it was the weight gain caused by more insulin use. People said it was this drug, it was that drug, it was lots of drugs prescribed together creating unknown interactions.

We had no idea whether any of these things were the reason. The coordinating center and investigators conducted additional analyses, but those analyses were not conclusive because they were not pre-specified, did not compare randomized groups, or were subject to multiple comparisons without statistical adjustment.

The only thing we could say with certainty was that the *strategy* of lowering glycemia to non-diabetic levels using multiple medications in people like those in ACCORD (middle-aged and older, average diabetes duration ten years, a third already with cardiovascular disease) did not prevent cardiovascular events and appeared to increase death rates.

After studying the results, the American Diabetes Association did modify their guidance for practice to recommend that physicians consider more modest glycemia targets for older patients at high risk.

The ACCORD lipid and blood pressure trials continued until

their planned end about a year and a half later. For the lipid trial, the combination therapy (fibrate plus statin) did *not* reduce cardiovascular events compared with a statin alone. For the blood pressure trial, the intensive lowering to a "normal" level of systolic pressure (less than 120), compared with a more standard treatment target (less than 140), also did *not* reduce the cardiovascular events, though it did significantly reduce strokes, which was not unexpected.

The control groups for the three ACCORD trials were the current standard of care—treatment strategies already proved to reduce cardiovascular disease risk in people with type 2 diabetes. Attacking these risk factors more intensively did not improve health outcomes. The NEJM editorial that accompanied the 2008 ACCORD results noted that only 10% of patients achieve the current goals. So, it seems we should be paying more attention to achieving the current goals, doesn't it?

Treating glycemia to a non-diabetic level did not negate the harmful effects of having diabetes. So perhaps the best way to reduce adverse effects of diabetes is to prevent the diabetes in the first place.

We know how to reduce rates of type 2 diabetes: lose weight, eat a healthy diet, and engage in regular physical activity. The Diabetes Prevention Program, a randomized trial in adults with pre-diabetes, proved the effectiveness of this approach.

So it seems we need both to achieve further attainment of current treatment goals for adults already with the disease, as well as prevent diabetes in those who do not already have it.

UNPREVENTABLE?

I search online to find out more about research on Parkinson's Disease, especially research pertinent to prevention. The National Institute of Neurological Disorders and Stroke (NINDS) website mentions several avenues of research relevant to prevention: the roles of various environments, genetics, stem cells, proteins, and nerve growth factors; identification of potential biomarkers or early symptoms that could predict who will be affected; and effects of the gut biome (all the microorganisms in our intestines, which, we are discovering, may be related to numerous diseases).

A recent breakthrough is related to the possible role of alpha-synuclein, a protein found in the brain that has aberrant forms (clumping or abnormal folding) in people with Parkinson's. Let's see if we can apply Hill's evidence of causality to abnormal alpha-synuclein:

• Association with Parkinson's: yes

• Dose-response relationship: unclear

• Temporal sequence (abnormal alpha-synuclein present before the disease): unclear

• Specificity: unclear (abnormal alpha-synuclein may affect other conditions; other factors may need to be controlled)

• Biological plausibility: yes (abnormal alpha-synuclein may be toxic to brain cells)

• Reducing abnormal alpha-synuclein reduces Parkinson's risk: unknown

There is a vaccine under development to attack clumping of the alpha-synuclein. Testing effects of such a vaccine would provide high-level evidence of whether abnormal alpha synuclein is indeed causal for Parkinson's.

These avenues of research seem very promising. But even if they find that abnormal alpha-synuclein plays a role, they still need to find out what causes the protein to become abnormal and clump.

There's evidence that exercise may help in secondary prevention —in other words, improve the symptoms in people who already have Parkinson's. And so, I wonder how my Parkinson's is related to my painful sciatica from a herniated disc that I had about the time my symptoms surfaced.

Here's my hypothesis: I fell because of Parkinson's symptoms in my left leg, which made me uncoordinated and clumsy. I hit my knee hard on the concrete, and the collision transferred to my spine, so a disc in my lower back herniated—because I already had spine problems, like most 60-year-olds. The herniated disc pressed on the nerve that goes down my leg, causing terrible pain in my buttocks and leg, called sciatica.

Then I couldn't exercise at all. (I could barely walk.) And my Parkinson's symptoms emerged.

Here is a "logic model" showing the causal chain:

Mild Parkinson's' symptoms ——→ uncoordinated leg ——→ fall ——→ herniated disk ——→ sciatic pain ——→ no exercise ——→ more Parkinson's symptoms

I tell my neurologist about this notion. He says it's plausible since exercise is useful in managing Parkinson's symptoms. But the prevention aspect is less clear. Before I fell, I was teaching three hours of vigorous exercise a week and walking to work and back every day, 20 minutes each way. I'm convinced that this regimen was suppressing my Parkinson's symptoms.

Could exercise delay or reduce the deterioration of the neurons that make dopamine? In my medical training, I was taught that the brain, after it completes development, is pretty static—that neurons can't be replaced, that damage is irreversible. But now experts think that the brain is amenable to change—that there is neuroplasticity. The hypothesis is that exercise could remodel brain tissue to form alternate pathways to (perhaps only partially) compensate for the damaged ones.

Many studies about exercise and Parkinson's—in humans and animals—support the notion that regular exercise is beneficial for Parkinson's and can help reduce symptoms. But the ideal exercise regimen is unknown. Is one type of exercise better than others? How long and often do you need to exercise?

I need to get back to exercising. I went for six months without exercising at all after my fall, as my herniated disc repaired itself. Now, I have to start all over and build up my fitness.

I don't go back to step aerobics because I'm afraid of falling off the step, and, because of months being sedentary, I'm not even fit enough to do it now.

But I can exercise at home. I have dumbbells, a yoga mat, exercise bands. There are lots of exercises I can do with this equipment—I know them because I used to teach classes using them. So I exercise at home: squats, abductor extensions, lunges, and bridges for lower body; overhead presses, bicep curls, and triceps kickbacks for upper body; crunches and "supermans" for core; and others.

I buy an exercise bike with a small footprint that fits in the corner of our bedroom—a "spinning" bike, where you can stand up and pedal to get a good aerobic workout. At first, I can bike for only five minutes at a time—I get too tired to bike longer. But I do go back to walking to work again as many days as possible. Fifteen to twenty minutes each way gives me at least the 150 minutes of moderate intensity physical activity a week recommended in the 2008 Physical Activity Guidelines for Americans.

I don't think walking is vigorous enough, however, so I've decided to do my own study of vigorous exercise. First, I need to build up my fitness so I can do vigorous exercise again. I will be the only participant—it's a single-subject non-randomized experiment. Non-blinded, of course.

PART 8: SCIENCE MANAGEMENT

"To manage is to forecast and plan, to organize, to command, to coordinate and to control."

—Henri Fayol, 1916

It's Confusing

"Thanks for taking time to look at the study idea I emailed you," said the assistant professor on the phone. Helping potential grant applicants, often over the phone, was part of my job from 1992 until 2009. "When is an RFA going to come out on that topic?" I had to answer this question more times than I could count. A Request for Applications (or funding opportunity announcement) from NIH specified a research area of interest and an amount of funding available.

"You don't need to wait for an RFA on your topic. You can just submit an application," I replied

"Really? I thought I had to wait for an RFA!"

"A lot of people think that, but 75 percent of our funding isn't in response to an RFA. It's for investigator-initiated applications. Unsolicited."

"So if there's no RFA, how do I know what kind of research NHLBI wants?"

"Well, I can tell you that NHLBI wants excellent research on heart, lung, and blood topics. Explore our website, and you will see many examples of our funding."

"That's great. I'll do that! What did you think about my study concept?" she asked.

"Well, the general topic about the effects of physical activity on cardiovascular disease risk factors makes sense. But having four different intervention groups probably won't do well in peer review—reviewers like simpler studies. So I suggest focusing it more—maybe only test the most promising intervention and compare that to a control group. Also, it would be helpful to identify a single primary outcome. As it is now, you want to measure so many things that it's hard to figure out what your main question is."

"So which intervention do you think I should test?" she asked.

"That depends on your specific research question. What do you want to know? A good research question includes several pieces: what intervention (or exposure), compared to what control (or comparison), in what people, on what outcome. You'll have to do more work to clarify your research question. Whatever you decide, you have to justify it based on prior evidence and public health needs."

"I understand. So do you think I'm senior enough to be the PI?"

"A principal investigator needs to be someone with enough experience to lead the study. Based on what you sent me, you are proposing something very complicated. If you reduce the scope and complexity, so it's more manageable, you may be qualified to be PI since you do have some research experience and quite a few publications. If you decide to come in as PI, I recommend having more senior people on your team, but make sure they're actually involved in the application and the study. It's pretty obvious to peer reviewers when someone's name is just tacked on, and the text doesn't reflect their expertise."

"Okay." She said. "I'll discuss this with my department chair. What can you tell me about peer review?"

"Well, I can suggest a peer review group, and you can request your application be assigned to that group in your cover letter. I can go to the review meeting to hear what they say. But I'm in what's called 'program,' and I can't influence the review." I was always careful to avoid the perception that I could influence what was funded, because I couldn't. "The separation between program and review is like the separation between church and state."

"Oh," she replied. "I thought you could put a good word in for my study, since you're interested in physical activity."

"Well, it doesn't work that way. Each application gets a priority score and a percentile ranking based on peer review. Then NHLBI lists the studies in order by percentile and funds all the studies down to a certain cutpoint—called the pay-line—that can be afforded by the budget."

This approach was more hands-off than how some other institutes worked; some did jump around to fund studies "of interest." I was proud of the way our institute did it, though, because it prevented an "old boys' network" where who you knew was more important than what was in your application. Plus there were a lot of differences of opinion amongst staff as to what's important to fund.

"Is there any other advice you can give me?"

"I suggest looking at successful grant applications to see how they're written. Try to get one or two from a senior investigator in your institution. The specific aims have to be clear, and the rest of the application should have sections that match back to each of the aims."

"Okay. Wow, this sounds like a lot of work. Thanks for your help."

"Sure. Let me know when you plan to submit it and the exact title, and I'll request it be assigned to our program group at NHLBI."

"I thought you said it would be assigned to a peer review group."

"Well, yes. It's assigned to two places: a review group for the review, and a program group for funding and follow-up."

"Oh. That's a bit confusing."

"Yes, it is, isn't it?"

But We Have Guidelines

I sat in a chair at the back of a hotel conference room, attending a peer-review meeting for another study about physical activity. This particular meeting was in 1995 or so. I was there to observe the review of a proposed study to compare the effects of different physical activity regimens on blood pressure, blood cholesterol, and body weight. It would be a large, multi-center study and had already made it through the institute's 500K policy, which stated that an NIH Institute must agree to accept for review (though not necessarily to fund) any application costing more than $500,000 in direct costs in one or more years. (A few years later I was part of our division's 500K decision-making process, and I admit I was a sieve. In other words, I wanted to let almost all of them in—I believed they should be allowed to go to peer review. Another woman in the process was a wall—she didn't want to accept any of them; she usually won.)

"Let's move on to the physical activity application," the chairman announced.

"Well, I don't think it'll take much time," one of the committee members offered. "We shouldn't recommend funding it." I saw on the attendance list that the speaker was in a different field, hematology I think, and wasn't an assigned reviewer for the study. "We don't need any more physical activity studies, because we already have guidelines."

What? I nearly fell off my chair.

We didn't have official federal guidelines, but we did have recommendations from the Centers for Disease Control, the American College of Sports Medicine, and other groups. I knew the recommendations well—moderate-intensity aerobic activity, like brisk walking, for 30 minutes 5 days a week to improve your overall health; or 20-30 minutes of vigorous exercise three times a week to improve aerobic fitness. But recommendations aren't supposed to squelch additional research. There was a lot we didn't know about the effects of physical activity.

I debated silently with myself about speaking up, and I lost. I didn't say anything. I had been told not to interfere with peer review. Although the committee member wasn't an expert in the field—and wasn't even assigned to be a reviewer of that application—she swayed the committee. The application didn't get a fundable score.

I was supposed to advise the applicant about what to do next, but darned if I knew. I ended up telling him to look at the reviewers' comments on the summary statement. And then to keep trying, as persistence often pays off. Oh, and to simplify the study and bring the cost down.

Often the most experienced professionals don't agree to be peer reviewers. Academics with less experience may take on the task to learn about the process and what it takes to have a successful application. That is one reason some people think NIH peer review is "broken." Despite glitches like this one, however, I think peer review is one of the best things that NIH does. Who better to judge the quality of a proposed study than experts in the field? The review committee chair, however, needs to assure that non-experts—as in this case—don't mess up the process.

Herding Cats

"Our goal is to take over a thousand pages that summarize the scientific evidence about the relationship between physical activity and a dozen different health conditions and boil it down to short, action-oriented recommendations," our writing group chairman told us. "This won't be an easy task." It was 2007, and I was at a meeting of about twenty government experts invited to be on a writing group for the first official federal *Physical Activity Guidelines for Americans.*

An expert panel convened a couple of years prior by the Department of Health and Human Services had reviewed existing scientific evidence about physical activity and a broad range of health problems, from arthritis to mental health, from cancer to heart disease. They had written a report summarizing the available evidence. Now our writing group of federal scientists and public-health experts was supposed to translate that evidence into recommendations for the public. These guidelines would be stronger than recommendations from various professional groups, as they would drive federal government positions, education, and programs.

There were many issues to consider. Should the recommendations be for disease prevention in basically healthy people, or should they also be for people who already have health conditions? How can recommendations cut across the various health topics and age groups? How should recommendations be worded so they are clear? Is there a minimum amount of activity that should be recommended; if so, what is it?

We deliberated all day, reached a decision on one or two issues, and adjourned for the day. Then the next morning, members wanted to revisit the decisions. This happened day after day for most of the week. We were getting nowhere.

I wondered how I could help. So I plotted on a graph the range of minutes (least to most) of moderate activity (like walking) associated with reduced risk (compared with being sedentary) for each of 11 health conditions reviewed in the evidence report.

From least to most physical activity needed, they came out in this order: fall prevention, hip fracture prevention, daily functioning, bone health, mental health, overall mortality, metabolic health (e.g., diabetes), arthritis, heart health, cancer prevention, and weight loss. (Note that weight loss required the most physical activity.) Amazingly, the graph revealed that 150 minutes per week of moderate-intensity aerobic activity (equivalent to brisk walking) compared to being sedentary, was associated with a lower risk for all the conditions!

Hardly any of these studies were randomized trials, but they were the evidence that we had. I shared the graph with the chairman and the group.

"We are making very slow progress on the guidelines," said the chairman toward the end of an intense week. "So I'm going to take these discussions under advisement and come back with some draft recommendations." If the chairman hadn't taken over, I'm not sure we would have had anything to release.

So the *2008 Physical Activity Guidelines for Americans* recommended at least 150 minutes a week of moderate-intensity aerobic activity (like brisk walking), or 75 minutes a week of vigorous activity (like running), or (unlike prior recommendations) an equivalent combination, at least 10 minutes at a time spread out over the week. The guidelines were intended to be flexible to give people options; this approach was consistent with the evidence, as different studies looked at different ways people could be active.

The examples below (which I created—there are many more examples in the guidelines themselves) meet or exceed the recommendations:

- Walking at a brisk pace (say 20 minutes per mile) for 30 minutes five days a week—a total of 150 minutes of moderate-intensity activity for the week.
- Riding a bicycle casually for an hour 3 times a week (120 minutes of moderate-intensity) plus mowing your lawn for an hour once a week (another 60 minutes of moderate activity)—a total of 180 minutes of moderate activity for the week.
- Social dancing two hours on a weekend (120 minutes of moderate activity) plus lifting weights for an hour midweek (60 minutes of moderate activity)—a total of 180 minutes of moderate activity for the week.
- Running 30 minutes three times a week—a total of 90 minutes of vigorous activity for the week.

The point is to find something that works for you, because the best exercise is, as they say, the exercise you will actually do.

The report also said, in a bow to people who are pretty sedentary, that if you can't do the recommended 150 minutes per week of moderate activity, at least do something because some physical activity is better than none. This was an extrapolation of the evidence, but we believed it to be true. So we can add to the above examples walking down the block and back for 15 minutes after dinner three times a week—a total of 45 minutes for the week.

From the existing evidence, it would not be wrong to conclude that physical activity has broad salutary effects on many health parameters, making it, as I heard someone say once and adopted myself, "the closest thing we have to a fountain of youth."

Being on this guideline group was a good experience for me, but I failed to learn a valuable lesson that I could have used later: If you want a project to be completed, sometimes you have to take it into your own hands, as the chair of this committee did.

Supervision & Politics

J eff, who had hired me and then moved up to be the program director, stepped into a different role as a senior scientific advisor to the division director—a transition step, it seemed, to his retirement. So I applied for his program director job, and I got it.

In my new position, I was responsible for overseeing three supervisors who in turn supervised 15 doctoral-level professional staff members. The portfolio for the program was about 250 research grants and 17 multi-center studies, totaling about $190 million in annual funding. I got a new office, and finally, after a decade at NIH, some new office furniture.

It wasn't the first time I had supervised supervisors, but it was the first time I had to supervise people who had previously been my peers. My philosophy was to be their collaborator and work with them to try and get their requests approved, rather than tell them what to do—the latter approach being common at NIH (though it didn't have to be that way).

Peter K, one of the research group leaders who had been at the Institute for decades, was interested in the physiology of behaviors as related to health, such as the effects of stress and depression on heart attacks. I was more interested in behaviors as defined as what people actually do—like what they eat, how much and type of physical activity they get, whether they smoke. But I agreed with him that both areas were important to study. Peter K was quite successful over the years.

Mike D, the other research group leader, was an interventional cardiologist—his clinical work was to "drop a line" into a patient's coronary artery and insert a stent (a little wire cage) to keep the artery open if there was narrowing or a heart attack. He held a part-time practice in the "cath lab" at a local hospital and kept his finger on the pulse (literally) of what cardiologists wanted to know.

One day Mike D came to my office carrying a thick three-ring binder and sat down at my meeting table to brief me on all the studies in his research group. I could easily follow the study design issues but needed to learn some cardiology. What did I know about implantable cardioverter defibrillators? What did I know about percutaneous coronary intervention? What did I know about the different types of diuretics and their use in heart failure? Not much. So Mike taught me some cardiology. I was responsible for assuring all his group's studies were functioning well, so I attended all their DSMB (Data and Safety Monitoring Board) meetings.

I developed a good working relationship with both Peter K and Mike D. They would drop in to see me with this idea or that idea. I tried to help their ideas through the process, mainly by asking them questions and editing write-ups to be a bit more accessible to people outside their fields.

As NIH is a federal agency, we weren't immune to federal politics. When Bill Clinton was president (1993-2001), he charged Al Gore with "reinventing government," which included reducing the number of government employees. During George W. Bush's administration (2001-2009) the Republicans in power doubled the NIH budget. So from 1993 to 2009, fewer staff members were available, yet more grants had to be overseen, and, at the same time, more administrative burden was added for each grant.

For example, one of our responsibilities was to assure that

funded grants were enrolling enough participants into their studies. That included a new requirement that the gender and race/ethnicity distributions in the study would be similar to the population of the US. We got quarterly recruitment reports from the investigators of each study, met internally to discuss those whose recruitment was lagging, and then contacted the investigators to find out their issues and maybe offer a suggestion or two. If recruitment was so slow that they couldn't get their research done, we could cancel a grant award. That happened very rarely.

In 2009, when Congress passed President Obama's ARRA (American Recovery and Reinvestment Act), NIH got a bolus of money that we had to pass through to research institutions to stimulate the economy. NIH had to figure out how to move research funding much faster than the process typically worked.

So NIH established a mechanism for administrative supplements—extra funding to add additional scientific efforts to existing grants—and developed new ARRA-specific requests for applications (RFAs). Those of us in "program" brainstormed topics for these RFAs; I sent in a few topics about applied clinical research that made it into the final list. We received and reviewed numerous requests, progress reports, and applications, over and above the usual workload, but with no increase in staffing to do the extra work.

Then in 2013, the Obama administration put in place "sequestration," which reduced funding to numerous federal agencies, including NIH. And now, in 2019, the Trump budget proposes even more cuts to NIH.

So despite a period of budget increases, we were always under the stress of needing to meet more and more administrative demands without an increase in the number of staff members. We worked our butts off.

Implementation Studies

When I took Jeff's old position as program director, I wanted to make some changes in the program. I was interested in funding more implementation studies: practical studies in real-life settings that examine approaches to getting into practice what we already know is good for your health. For example, only about half of adults with hypertension have their blood pressure controlled to recommended levels. How to achieve higher rates of control not only involves patient adherence to prescribed treatments, but also involves provider behaviors (such as prescribing medications), system strategies (such as performance standards in hospitals and clinics), or policy changes (such as insurance reimbursements).

I'd been interested in these types of studies since working on handbooks for health departments in Texas and finding little research examining the effects of various implementation strategies at organizational or community levels. So I proposed reorganizing my program of three research groups— just moving people around really—to create a research group for implementation research. We were funding several studies of this ilk anyway, but a new research group would give them a home. It took me two years to get the reorganization approved. I hired Larry, a preventive medicine physician who was working elsewhere at NIH, to lead the new group.

We were moving along nicely with our new organizational

structure and developing new initiatives in implementation research, when a short year later, Betsy, our new institute director after Claude, invited me to a meeting with just the two of us. I sat down on her yellow sofa in her large office; she sat down in the facing armchair. She was blond and beautiful, smart and aloof.

"As you know, I am reorganizing the institute," she told me. "Congratulations, you're going to be the Branch Chief for the Clinical Applications and Prevention Branch."

This came as a complete surprise. I knew Betsy was going to reorganize the institute, but I didn't know the details. In this new position, I would no longer be supervising supervisors, and she was doing away with the new implementation research group. In fact, she was eliminating the research group level completely and moving Mike D's entire cardiology group to another division. What did she mean by saying congratulations? She hadn't asked me whether I wanted this position. It felt like a demotion.

And even more changes were in the works. Peter S was stepping down as our division director. He was my supervisor, the position was only one step higher in the hierarchy for me, and I was a logical internal candidate. I applied for the job, made it to the short list, and had an interview. But I didn't get it. Betsy hired a cardiologist from outside NIH. I felt like Hillary Clinton in 2008—ready and primed and in line to be the next person for the position, and in comes Barack Obama—I mean Mike L, young, energetic, charismatic, smart, and now my supervisor.

I felt like I had been demoted when I no longer was supervising supervisors, my implementation research group had been discarded, I felt disrespected because I hadn't even been asked if I wanted the branch chief job (and I wasn't sure I wanted it), and I didn't get the division director job. So I decided to step away from the administrative headaches and, following for the third time into Jeff's shoes, I became a senior scientific advisor for the division—a non-supervisory position.

I continued working on the ACCORD study. I also became

the obesity maven for the institute, developing and leading an institute-wide obesity working group. I spent more time on implementation research, including initiating a new study that would look at effects of anti-obesity programs and policies in communities, and I developed and held a working group of experts to advise the institute on implementation research and practice, focusing on prevention.

"Welcome to this workshop on improving the delivery of preventive interventions in clinical practice," I said to the thirty workshop attendees whom we had invited, all experts in relevant fields. "NHLBI has a history of leadership in implementation research and in efforts to move scientific findings into practice. We have funded research on patient adherence, hypertension control, clinical interventions to reduce obesity and physical inactivity, and systems approaches to improve the delivery of guideline-based care. Our goal in this workshop is to consider what we have learned from these efforts and develop recommendations both for practice and for additional research."

"Patients and clinicians often think differently about chronic treatment regimens," said one of the workshop co-chairs, in introductory comments. "There is a role for education—of patients and of clinicians—and also a role for changing environments."

The other workshop co-chair, noted, "It's not sufficient to stop doing research after we identify efficacious strategies and assume the strategies will actually be delivered in practice. We also need to study how to achieve effectiveness in real-world settings, how to improve implementation of strategies shown to be successful."

Attendees gave presentations and discussed topics such as patient adherence, clinician adoption of evidence-based care, health-care teams, and collaborations between clinical sites and communities. By the end of two days, workshop attendees had come up with a substantial list of recommendations for practice and also recommendations for additional research. They recommended more practice-based and pragmatic studies, studies of medical systems, and studies of partnerships between the clinical and community settings. We published the report on the NHLBI website. In retrospect, I wish we had submitted the report to a scientific journal for publication. (Someone once advised me to publish everything you do. Good advice I wish I had taken.)

I could have stayed in the senior advisor position working on implementation research. But another position had opened up, one that was more about the practice side of things. It would be a move up for me—director of a division for the "application of research discoveries." That division was in the process of updating clinical practice guidelines on hypertension, cholesterol, and obesity, and it developed and implemented several national educational and awareness programs on heart, lung, and blood topics.

Translating scientific findings into recommendations for practice was a key purpose in the position. Whoever took the position would lead the division that developed clinical practice guidelines and implemented nation-wide educational programs. It seemed like a position I had been working toward my entire career. So I applied.

Lifestyle Lecture

T o introduce my 2009 talk about heart disease prevention, I told the NIH audience the story of Grabwell
Grommett, which I had been using for decades after I
encountered it being told and retold in the prevention field. I
did not make this story up, but I did modify it. I illustrated each
point with photos or clip-art on PowerPoint slides.

Here is the story of Grabwell Grommett as I told it to my
audience:

*Grabwell Grommett was a middle-aged man who worked
long hours in a very stressful job. One night after an exhausting
day, he had a nightmare—he saw a banner stretched across the
sky that said, "Grabwell Grommett, someone is trying to kill
you."*

*He woke with a start and sat up in bed, waking up his
wife, Portia. She said, "What's the matter, dear?" He replied
that he had a bad dream. He lay back down but was unable to go
back to sleep.*

*At breakfast—which was his usual fried eggs, bacon, and
coffee with heavy cream—he told her about the dream. She said,
"Don't worry dear, it was just a dream. I'm sure nobody is trying to kill you."*

*He went to work as usual, but the day was so busy with
the phone ringing and meeting after meeting and a huge pile
of paperwork to get through that he didn't have time to give it
another thought. But he did think about it all the way home,*

driving an hour in heavy traffic, while he smoked.

His wife consoled him that evening, greeting him with his usual martini as he entered the door. While serving him his second helping of beef stroganoff at dinner, she told him again not to worry, that it was just a dream. After his third martini, he went to bed late as usual and got his usual four hours of sleep.

The years passed, and Grabwell took pleasure in knowing that whoever was trying to kill him, hadn't done so yet. Then late one evening, while sitting at his desk at work, death did come to Grabwell Grommett, as it comes to us all.

His wife, Portia, demanded a full autopsy. The autopsy showed a massive heart attack, signs of a previous stroke, cirrhosis of the liver, and a small lung cancer.

"I'm so relieved," she said, "he died of natural causes."

I was giving this talk for a worksite wellness series where all NIH staff members were invited—janitors, assistants, doctors, nurses, NIH leadership. I had given similar talks before, once for a lecture series open to the local community called "Medicine for the Public." I loved doing these kinds of talks, where I showed some scientific data to illustrate the basis for actions we can all take to help reduce our risk of heart disease.

"Now everybody, stand up," I said. The 50 or so people in the audience all stood. "Now get ready:

- "Sit down if you smoke. [Only a few people sat down]
- "Sit down if you can't remember the last time you got your blood cholesterol checked. [A few more sat down]
- "Sit down if you don't know what your blood pressure is. [Several more sat down]
- "Sit down if you don't exercise at least three days a week [A few more sat down]
- "Sit down if you don't eat five servings of fruits and vegetables a day. [Almost everybody else sat down.]

• "Sit down if you have gained more than ten pounds since you were in your 20s." [Only one person remained standing: Michael, the man who had invited me to give the talk—the head of the fitness center.]

"Let's give Michael a round of applause," and we all clapped for Michael. "Sure, these things are hard to do, but they are all things you CAN do—if you put your mind to it, as Michael has."

I told the audience I was going to tell them how to prevent the leading cause of death in the nation: cardiovascular disease. That included paying attention to blood pressure, blood cholesterol, body weight, diet, and physical activity—risk factors for cardiovascular diseases, which are all related to each other.

I defined hypertension—blood pressure over 140/90 mm of mercury—then showed slides of data on how we know that hypertension increases the risk of cardiovascular diseases, especially stroke.

I briefly described ways to lower blood pressure, showing data from a meta-analysis that combined results of 25 randomized trials. The results showed that people who are overweight or obese could reduce their elevated blood pressure by losing only about 5 percent of their body weight. Another meta-analysis combined results of 72 randomized trials and showed that exercise reduces blood pressure in people whether or not they have hypertension.

And of course, I showed the results of the DASH studies about how a dietary pattern and reducing dietary sodium can lower elevated blood pressure.

I also talked about blood cholesterol and how eating foods with lower saturated fats can help keep your blood cholesterol in check. If diet doesn't help your blood cholesterol, exercise and losing weight could help. And medications (statins) are very effective.

Then I showed them how to read a nutrition label on packaged foods, projecting some labels on the screen and going over the different pieces of information.

"Now we're going to have audience participation," I said. "I need two volunteers."

Two women raised their hands, and I invited them up to the front of the room.

"Okay, it's time for lunch," I said, "and you need something to drink. Here are two choices." I opened a paper bag, pulled out a 16-ounce bottle of regular coke and a 16-ounce bottle of orange juice, and handed one to each of the women.

"Let's say you want to hold your calorie intake down to control your weight," I said. "So which drink should you choose?"

They looked at the labels on the bottles. "You can look at each other's together," I said, which they did. "Let's give them a minute," I said to the audience. "But you can see copies of the labels on the screen behind me." In a minute or so, the women said they were ready. "Okay, then, which drink do you pick?" I asked.

"Well, the orange juice is better for you, and it has half the calories, so we pick the OJ," said one of the women. A murmur arose from the audience.

"Does anybody in the audience have anything to say?" I asked. Another woman had raised her hand. "Yes, you, stand up so we can all hear you."

"The OJ has two servings in that bottle," she said. The women at the front of the room looked again at the bottle of OJ. "Oh, yeah," said one. "We missed that. The two bottles have the same number of calories, if you drink the whole bottle."

"Very good," I said. "The OJ and coke have the same number of calories if you drink the whole bottle. So here's what you really should drink." I opened the paper bag again, pulled out two bottles of water, and handed one to each of the women. They laughed along with the audience.

"Thanks for helping us out. You can keep the water," I said. "Let's give them a round of applause.

"Now everybody, stand up again and let's do another exercise. Some actual moderate intensity exercise! Just stay where you are, in front of your chairs."

I started playing some music with a good beat and said,

"Okay, march in place," which we all did. We kept marching, lifting arms to the ceiling, lifting knees high. It was a lot of fun. At least they looked like they were having fun—I know I was.

"That's what moderate-intensity activity feels like," I said after the song was over. "The recommendation is to do 150 minutes a week of moderate physical activity. It could be 30 minutes each day for five days, or 50 minutes for three days, or other combinations. And it could be aerobics like we just did, or walking, or mowing your lawn, or washing your car. Biking or bowling. Dancing or vacuuming.

"Do you know what the best exercise is?" I asked rhetorically. I paused and looked around the room. "It's the one you will do," I answered, smiling.

"All these lifestyle changes may be hard for you," I concluded. "But they do make a difference. It's hard, I know, but you can do them if you try.

"Thanks for your attention."

The audience applauded. Several women (why is it always women?) came up to talk with me afterward to tell me their stories. I wanted to do more work like this. I waited to find out about my application for the division director for the "application of research discoveries."

MY NEW LIFE

About a year before my Parkinson's diagnosis, before I fell and my symptoms started, Bruce and I had sold our house in the suburbs and moved into a condominium in a more urban area. Now we can walk to NIH, two metro stations, restaurants, grocery stores, movies, and shops. Our condo has no stairs and is accessible by elevator. The building has a ramp that leads to a door with a handicap door opener. And I have long-term care insurance because I want Bruce to have those resources to take care of me if needed.

So, somehow, we planned for my condition even before I was diagnosed. After my father got his ALS diagnosis, he put hand controls in his car, got an electric scooter, had his downstairs bathroom remodeled for accessibility, and moved his bedroom to the first floor. We were always trying to stay ahead of his condition. I'm glad we prepared sooner than he did—before anything special is needed.

I'm on a simplified medication regimen that works very well, as long as I take the meds exactly on time, four times a day. But I do feel a bit shaky on my feet and uncoordinated even when medicated.

I worry about falling again, so I give away of all my shoes that are heels or slides and replace them with low-heeled shoes with straps or laces. Sometimes I think I look like a dork going to work in my Mary Jane shoes with flat heels, rounded toes, and a strap. But at least the *meds are good enough that I don't need to use a cane.*

I have some trouble with fine motor actions like buttoning buttons, fastening necklaces, and putting in earrings. I'm glad I can still type.

It helps to think of the Parkinson's as a chronic disease that can be treated but not cured, like arthritis, diabetes, or heart disease.

So I'm coping pretty well.

I have a new routine. I wake up early—not on purpose, I just wake up. I look at the beautiful sunrise from our East-facing 12th-floor condo apartment, take a photo of the sunrise and post it on my Facebook page to say good morning to all my friends.

I take my morning medications, do 10 to 20 minutes of moderate exercises in our second bedroom where I have dumbbells and a yoga mat, shower, get dressed, eat breakfast, put on my Mary Jane shoes, fix my hair and makeup...and leave to face the day at work.

In my new position, I have a great opportunity to make a difference. I'm not going to let the Parkinson's stop me.

PART 9: FROM EVIDENCE TO PRACTICE

"We want progress in medicine to be clear and unequivocal, but of course it rarely is."

—Atul Gawande,

Complications: A Surgeon's Notes on an Imperfect Science, 2002

A New Position

I walked into our institute director's large, and recently re-decorated, office suite wearing a lovely flowered dress, a color-coordinated suit jacket, and my new patent-leather red peep-toe shoes that my daughter picked out for me. (You don't have any cool shoes like these, Mom; try them on, she had said.) The receptionist waved me in, "Go on in. She's waiting for you."

Sitting behind her desk in the middle of the large office, a wall of windows at her left, Betsy looked up from her centrally placed desk. She wore a yellow suit matching her coiffed blonde hair. She stood up, walked around the desk in her high heels (sans stockings), and shook my hand. "Welcome to your new job. Let's go meet your staff." Then she walked me down the long hallway to a conference room where my new division was waiting to meet their new director—me. It was November 2009.

When I had taught prevention with Dr. Sherwin 20 years earlier, we had the students read about studies that resulted in the *National High Blood Pressure Education Program* and *the National Cholesterol Education Program*. The programs had enlisted multiple organizations across the nation in a common goal of improving the public's health based on scientific evidence. Their actions had changed the face of preventive medical care across the nation, and even the world, by developing and promoting clinical practice guidelines based on scientific evidence. Those programs may be why your doctor is interested in your blood pressure and your blood cholesterol!

Very few NIH institutes had significant efforts in translating evidence into practice, and none were as prominent as NHLBI's. These efforts were the main reason many of us had come to work at the NHLBI. We had Claude to thank. Now Betsy had changed the administrative structure so it was a division rather than an office, which elevated its importance.

Being director of the division for the application of research discoveries at NHLBI was the highest level to which I aspired, as far as I wanted to get. President Obama would now be my boss's, boss's, boss's, boss (only four bosses this time; before it was seven). In this job, I thought I could really contribute to improving the nation's health!

The search committee, eight high-level people who worked at NIH, most of whom I knew, had interviewed me together about a month earlier in a small windowless conference room on the NIH campus. It seemed they had a list of questions and were taking turns going down the list. "Tell us about yourself." "What experience have you had that has prepared you for this job?" "What do you see as the goals for the division?" "Describe for us a situation that was difficult to handle, and how you handled it." "What do you see as your strengths and weaknesses?" "Why do you want this job?"

I answered all their questions as best I could, and then said, "I would love to be the new division director. I think it's the perfect job for me at this stage of my career."

Later, when Betsy offered me the job, she said, "I want you to bring more science to this division. I'm sure you can do that."

"Yes, of course. That's exactly what I want to do," I had replied.

Now she was walking me into the conference room where the division staff members waited. I held my breath as she said,

"I'm pleased to announce that Dr. Simons-Morton is your new division director."

Looking around at the twenty or so people sitting at the big oval table, I saw recognition in many faces. I knew about half of them and had worked on projects with a few.

Betsy left the room to let me interact with my new staff members. After I sat down, Rob—an African-American who had served as interim division director, and someone I respected a lot—introduced each person at the table, mentioning their projects.

"Karen you know. She's our obesity expert. She works on obesity prevention programs and obesity-related policy as well as the project to update the obesity guidelines.

"Jim you also know. He's our cholesterol expert and is working on updating the cholesterol guidelines.

"Eduardo, I think you also know him, is a physician coordinating the update of the blood pressure guidelines.

"Janet is a nutritionist. As nutrition coordinator for the institute, she reviews drafts of all governmental materials about nutrition—to make sure they're consistent with the U.S. Dietary Guidelines.

"Matilde is in charge of our community health worker program, which provides educational materials and support to community groups to reduce health disparities in communities of need."

These were only some of the people and the projects. The work was interesting, exciting, and important! It was exactly what I wanted to work on at this stage of my career. In a way, it would take me full circle to the handbooks we had written when I was in Texas—looking at the scientific evidence and translating it into action steps to improve public health—but at a much higher level, nationally.

"I'm delighted to be here," I told them. "Some of you know I've focused on studies that have direct relevance to practice. I think it's important to take evidence the next step—so it informs clinical and public health practice and makes a difference!" There was nodding all around.

"We'll have regular staff meetings to share information and discuss issues, and I'll set up a suggestion box—no need to put your name on any suggestions you drop into it. And please, stop by and check in with me now and then, or if you have issues or questions. I have an open-door policy. Except," I added, smiling, "well, except when my door is closed."

"Now, tell me more about yourselves..."

The primary way the division got work done was through government contracts that supported various organizations to do work overseen by our staff. The work included things like reviewing findings from scientific studies, writing summary reports, organizing meetings and workshops, writing educational materials, and setting up and maintaining educational websites.

After a few weeks, after I got a good feel for the contracts, I shared information with my staff: "Here's a handout summarizing all of our contracts—their purpose, duration, cost, and staff member in charge."

"We've never seen this information before," said one staff member. "Thanks so much for showing it to us!"

"Yeah, it's great not being in the dark anymore," said another.

"Well, we're a team," I replied. "You all should know what's going on in the division."

I discovered that the authority within the division had been centralized, with decision-making held close to the chest by leadership. But I wanted to give staff more responsibilities. So I told them, "I'm going to pay for all professional staff to be trained as project officers. So you can be in charge of projects. It'll also help you with your government careers."

"You're going to pay?"

"Well, it'll come out of the division budget—not my pocket. I've checked, and we can afford it."

Arriving at work in the morning, I would walk down the long hall onto which all our offices opened, stopping to ask each person what he or she was working on, how it was going, if there was any way I could help. I learned to do these "rounds" from Peter S. when I was in his division.

I loved my new job and my new division. We bonded in a shared vision.

A short time after I started in the position, however, Betsy left the institute, and I ended up working for someone other than the person I thought I'd be working for. I wish I had been given a heads up. But at the time, I didn't think it would make much of a difference. After all, I would be leading a division, and division directors have some authority over their division's directions. Don't they?

Too Much Salt?

P etite with long light-brown hair and a runner's physique, Janet peeked her head into my office in early 2010. "Do you have a minute? The DNC needs our input on sodium. HHS is updating the DGAs, and has to make some decisions," she said.

"The DNC? The Democratic National Committee?"

"Ha ha. No. Not that DNC. It's the NIH Division of Nutrition Coordination."

As the nutrition coordinator for our institute, Janet was aware of what was happening with government nutrition policy. NIH is part of the Department of Health and Human Services (HHS), which works with the Department of Agriculture to develop the Dietary Guidelines for Americans (DGAs). First published in 1980, the DGAs were the next step after the 1977 Dietary Goals for Americans that came from the "Senate Select Committee on Nutrition and Human Needs," led by Senator George McGovern. The DGAs are derived by examining the science relating nutrition to health.

The DGAs carry the force of policy—all government nutrition policies, like the nutrition labels on foods, and every government publication about diet, has to be consistent with the DGAs. As required by law, the government updates the DGAs every five years based on new scientific evidence. The 2010 update was being worked on when Janet came to talk with me.

"The expert committee report is out. But there are differences of opinion about what the sodium recommendation should be. They want our input."

"I know a fair amount about this topic, because I worked on DASH-Sodium," I replied.

"Yeah, that's one reason I'm asking. Do you have time to help?"

"Sure. What's the difference of opinion about?"

"Well, whether the DGAs should recommend eating the lowest sodium level tested in DASH-Sodium. Or whether the current recommendation of 2300 mg a day should be kept. So basically they're trying to decide between using 1500 or 2300 mg a day as a recommended maximum intake."

"Do you have the evidence report?"

"Yeah. I'll send you the link. It has the papers the committee looked at."

I scrolled through the scientific papers that the expert committee had reviewed and noticed that they focused on randomized trials examining the effects of changes in dietary sodium on blood pressure. Blood pressure is a risk factor for clinical events, like strokes, heart attacks, and kidney disease, which is the major reason we are interested in it. So why didn't the evidence review include studies with clinical events as outcomes? I asked Janet to help, and we located some very informative review papers of observational studies (not testing an intervention) that assessed associations between dietary sodium intake and cardiovascular events. These studies weren't looking only at whether dietary sodium affects blood pressure, but also whether it was associated with heart attacks and strokes.

Then we concisely summarized the body of evidence by categorizing it into four types of studies. We focused on cardiovascular outcomes, as cardiovascular disease is the leading cause of death in the U.S. Here's a summary of what we found:

- Category 1 (pretty low level of evidence)—observational studies that examine associations between dietary sodium and blood pressure level. Lots of studies.

• Category 2 (higher level of evidence)—observational studies that examine associations between dietary sodium and cardiovascular events, like heart attacks and strokes. A fair number of studies.

• Category 3 (high level of evidence for effects of sodium on blood pressure)—randomized trials examining effects of changes in sodium intake on blood pressure level. Lots of studies, including DASH-Sodium.

• Category 4 (highest level of evidence for effects of sodium on clinical events)—randomized trials examining effects of changes in sodium intake on cardiovascular events. Only one analysis, which was not the primary purpose of the study.

This is a typical situation when looking at epidemiology evidence: a lot of studies with the least robust evidence (categories 1-3), and a rare study with the most relevant and robust evidence (category 4). The expert panel had focused on category 3, whether lowering dietary sodium lowers blood pressure (which it does).

Because category 4 studies provide the highest level of evidence, we looked more closely at the single study in category 4. It was an analysis that combined results of two studies called the Trials of Hypertension Prevention (TOHP). These studies were randomized trials testing the effects of lowering dietary sodium (as well as other interventions like losing weight or meditating to reduce stress) on blood pressure.

Looking at cardiovascular events was not the original purpose of the TOHP studies, but the investigators had obtained follow-up information on the participants so they could analyze that outcome. The analysis revealed that the group who had lowered their dietary sodium also had significantly lower cardiovascular events compared with the group that had not reduced their sodium intake. Because information on cardiovascular disease wasn't available for all the participants, however, the findings were not as robust as they could have been.

"What level of sodium did they achieve in the lower sodium group in TOHP?" I asked Janet.

"I looked through the publications for that information. Guess what? The sodium level in the reduced sodium group was about 2400 mg/day."

"Really? That's the medium sodium level tested in DASH, not the lowest. Hmm... that doesn't give much support for the 1500 mg goal for the guidelines."

"Yeah. It's close to the previous recommendation."

We sent a brief "white paper" to the DNC and HHS, which described the four categories of studies. We were invited to meetings at the HHS in downtown D.C. at the Office of the Assistant Secretary of Health ("the ASH"). We met in the ASH's well-appointed classy conference room. The ASH, Dr. Koh, was there, along with his deputy, representatives from the CDC, and a representative from the Department of Agriculture (HHS and Agriculture were co-leads on the DGAs).

Dr. Koh welcomed everybody and told us that he'd like our input on how to resolve the sodium issue.

The CDC representative spoke first. "Here's a figure from the DASH-Sodium study," he said, passing handouts around the table. I recognized that figure—I had been using it in slides for years when I gave presentations about preventing heart disease. "These results show that eating 1500 mg/day of sodium lowers blood pressure compared with eating more than that. So we think that's the level that the DGAs should recommend."

Then it was my turn. "I agree DASH-Sodium found that lowering sodium intake to 1500 mg a day reduced blood pressure. But the folks in DASH-Sodium already had elevated blood pressure, so they don't represent the general population. And the study didn't look at cardiovascular events. There are lots of observational studies looking at sodium and CVD events, but we only found one randomized trial—an analysis of data from the Trials Of Hypertension Prevention. That analysis did find that lowering dietary sodium reduces CVD events, but the lower sodium level was about 2400 mg a day—close to the current recommendation, not near 1500 mg. So there is evidence we should lower our dietary sodium, but it isn't very strong that we should go as low as 1500 mg."

After the meeting, the ASH Deputy called me on my cell phone multiple times to ask what I thought of this or that study. He told me that the folks from the CDC provided the same study references as we did, but they had come to different conclusions. He was trying to understand why.

I tried to explain that some scientists are more conservative, saying you can't extrapolate beyond the type of people enrolled in a study or beyond the outcomes measured. Others are more liberal, in favor of a broader application of the principle behind the study results. It depends on whether you think a study is asking a specific question or is asking a conceptual question.

As an NIH representative, I thought it was my job to be as rigorous as possible. That meant interpreting evidence conservatively—not going beyond what the actual studies did and found. I had discussed the matter with my director, who had concurred with taking this approach.

The guidelines had to have a number, but, given the disagreements, it was still unclear which of the two numbers to pick. A compromise seemed to be in order. So the 2010 DGAs were written with two recommendations: limit daily sodium intake to 2300 mg for the general population (the same as the prior recommendation) and, for folks like the DASH-Sodium participants who had elevated blood pressure, limit daily intake to 1500 mg. In the DASH trial, as well as other studies, there was a greater effect of sodium lowering in African-Americans, so the 1500 mg/day was also recommended for that group.

It seemed like a good compromise. The 2010 DGAs were published and widely distributed. But the controversy continued. Which number should be used for the nutrient information on food labels? How can people reach the lower level when 75% of dietary sodium is from processed foods? These were policy issues, and I was not privy to discussions about them.

I felt like I had made a contribution, that I was doing what Betsy asked me to do when she hired me—bring more science to the division's activities. I felt good about being in this position, providing useful input, and conservatively interpreting scientific evidence as an NIH representative.

But I didn't pick up the phone and call the key proponents of the 1500 mg sodium level, even though I knew them. I went through the process as a government official, but not as a colleague. In retrospect, I wonder if that was the right way to proceed.

Each update of the DGAs has had its controversies. For 2010, as described above, the controversy was about dietary sodium. For the next revision (2015), the sodium recommendation remained essentially the same, but there was a controversy about dietary fats and cholesterol: The guideline authors had decided that the evidence around dietary cholesterol was insufficient to retain a previous, long-standing recommendation about limiting dietary cholesterol intake. (Keep in mind that dietary cholesterol and blood cholesterol are two different things. People always seem to get them confused.) High blood cholesterol is bad for your health, but saturated fat in the diet has more effect on blood cholesterol than does cholesterol in the diet.

Because the evidence standards had evolved, the committee dropped the recommendation about dietary cholesterol. The media had a field day, criticizing the scientists for always changing their minds.

Of course we should be able to change our minds! There is ever-accumulating data, and approaches to reviewing evidence change over time. We need to make the best recommendations possible given the available evidence, even if there are controversies. And there always will be controversies, because evidence is never complete.

To Screen Or Not

While "Snowmageddon" was blanketing the eastern U.S. in February 2010, with 40 inches of snow falling within a week, I sat at my kitchen table with my laptop computer, reading every word of the draft pediatric guidelines report. Occasionally I looked up specific studies online to check them. When the electricity went out and we lost our Wi-Fi connection, I packed up my computer, put my boots and parka on, and walked to a Starbucks about a mile away to continue my work.

"The pediatric guidelines are finished," Rae-Ellen had told me before she left our division to take a job outside of government. "The report was a lot of work. It includes blood cholesterol, blood pressure, nutrition, physical activity, smoking—all part of cardiovascular prevention that should start in childhood."

"Sounds great!" I replied. "I'm looking forward to reading it."

"I'll make sure you get a copy before I leave."

A panel of 14 experts convened by our institute had written the report with support from a half dozen institute staff, led by Rae-Ellen. I needed to read and approve the report because my division was responsible for it. With the government closed because of the snowstorm, I had time to give it a really good look.

I found it to be an excellent draft but missing some details and needing more justification in several places. Generally, in writing any report or scientific paper, it takes a lot of time to finalize the details, and this report was no exception. Staff in my division had given me a list of issues that arose when external reviewers had reviewed the draft report. Using that input as a guide, and adding some issues of my own, I gave the panel chair a list of issues to be addressed. And, although she was now working elsewhere, Rae-Ellen graciously donated her time to help finalize the report.

After fifteen months of working on all the details, and getting it through the NIH approval process, we finally released the pediatric guidelines report. One morning shortly after its release, Janet came to my office looking worried. "Folks at NIH aren't happy about the pediatric guidelines," she told me.

"Why?" I asked. "It's a good report."

"They aren't happy with the universal screening recommendation."

She was talking about a recommendation to test blood cholesterol in all children ages 9 to 11—every child, whether or not they had a family history of high cholesterol or heart disease, whether they were obese or thin, sedentary or active.

"But why?"

"It's controversial. And it's been in the news."

I was not surprised there were controversies in the report, as controversies often exist in clinical recommendations. My institute director had read and approved the report (and in fact had spoken quite highly of it), but should we have given the NIH director a personal heads up? In retrospect, that would have been a good idea. We should have known the media would report on it. They seem always to report on controversies.

Previous pediatric guidelines had recommended blood cholesterol testing in children with a family history of high cholesterol or cardiovascular disease. The new recommendation was broader—more children would be tested. Some people were saying that would cause children to be put on cholesterol-lowering medications for years, even for decades—a practice for which safety was unknown. But screening doesn't necessarily mean medications should be used. Knowing you have high blood cholesterol should be a signal to work on a healthier lifestyle, which can be very effective. (Ironically, the universal blood pressure screening recommendation didn't engender controversy, though issues are similar.)

The report noted that a fair proportion of children have high cholesterol even if they don't have a family history of elevated blood cholesterol or cardiovascular disease. These children were not even being tested under the prior recommendation. But since blood cholesterol "tracks"—if you have high cholesterol as a child you also are likely to have it later in life—the rationale to measure it early in life had seemed reasonable. The panel had seen comments on this issue from outside reviewers, but I didn't identify the recommendation as something we should discuss further, although Jim had mentioned it to me before he left for a position at another government agency (and he was right).

Why would it not be good to do a screening test? Wouldn't it be better to know, than not to know, if you have early disease? Or in this case, if you have a risk factor?

Unfortunately, physicians don't know whose test is falsely positive and whose test is truly positive. Since they can't ignore a positive test result, procedures may be done (like invasive biopsies) that can result in serious side effects. Treatments (including medications) also can cause serious side effects. So it's a balancing act between risk and benefit, with and without testing.

As you recall, in the course I taught about prevention, we calculated sensitivity and specificity of screening tests, and we noted some tricky issues in interpreting those test evaluations. But to really know how useful a screening test is, we need randomized trials looking at clinical outcomes—both beneficial and unfavorable—in people who receive the test compared with people who do not receive the test. Because screening is done in apparently healthy people, those studies need to be huge and of long duration so they can detect small differences in health outcomes. Also, investigators and study participants need to be willing to accept being assigned to not getting the test. And once conducted, how to interpret results is often controversial.

Examples of controversies you may have heard about include recommendations for mammography and for prostate-specific antigen to screen for breast and prostate cancers.

So the recommendation for universal screening of blood cholesterol in children was not alone in being controversial. Besides, assessing the effects of a screening test is more difficult in children than in adults (perhaps impossible), because of how long it takes from childhood to disease onset.

What could I, or should I, have done about the universal screening recommendation? Should I have asked the authors to change it? Should I have asked our institute director to get involved in the details and deal directly with the authors?

I wish I knew, because, contrary to what I thought at the time, the pediatric guidelines would not be the first new product released during my tenure as a division director—it would be one of only two new products released during my tenure as a division director.

Evidence Schmevidence

"What issues are on our agenda for today?" I asked, catalyzing a lively exchange among the half dozen people in the room. Shortly after I became a division director in 2009, I began chairing meetings of our staff who were working on the adult cardiovascular prevention guidelines. This project, organized and overseen by my division, had been set up to do something never done before: develop clinical practice guidelines for five topics simultaneously using the same methods. All the topics focused on preventing cardiovascular diseases in adults: high blood pressure, blood cholesterol, obesity, lifestyle, and risk assessment.

I don't remember who said what, or exactly the words, but our meetings went something like this:

"We'll have to carry forward some previous recommendations."

"We can't do that. We shouldn't include anything we don't do an updated evidence review on."

"But we can't do systematic reviews on everything—there are too many topics."

"We need to give guidance on all the issues."

I listened as they went back and forth, everybody weighing in.

"Whoa!" I said. "I see this is a hot topic! So let's see how this carry-forward issue plays out as we go forward. Right now, we need to finalize the systematic review methods. So what

263

methods issues do we need to address?"

Karen spoke up. "Blood pressure and cholesterol have a lot of randomized trials. But for obesity, we don't have trials on whether reducing weight will reduce CVD events."

"Good point," I replied. "There are a lot of observational studies but no trials. Are there any tools to evaluate the quality of observational studies?"

"There are assessment tools for randomized trials, but I'm not sure about observational studies," Eduardo said. "I'll look into it."

"Great. We could use Hill's evidence of causality to create a tool, if no tools exist," I offered.

Here's a bit of history about this project. Beginning in 1977, the National Heart, Lung, and Blood Institute (NHLBI) released several reports that contained evidence-based clinical practice guidelines for preventing cardiovascular diseases. These reports, written by expert panels convened by the institute, were a significant way to translate scientific evidence into clinical practice. The guidelines, which were widely adopted, focused on identifying and reducing three major risk factors: high blood pressure, high blood cholesterol, and obesity. Smoking, a critical risk factor, was addressed elsewhere by the federal government.

The first *Report of the Joint National Committee on Detection, Evaluation, and Treatment of High Blood Pressure* (JNC), released in 1977, set the stage for JNC 2 (1980) through JNC 7 (2004). The JNC reports were part of the *National High Blood Pressure Education Program (NHBPEP)*, comprising numerous organizations that influence clinical care and public health.

Each report added information or modified previous recommendations based on new research findings. JNC 1 recommended that patients with diastolic pressure above 105 receive "stepped-care" drug treatment, which adds medications over time until the blood pressure is reduced sufficiently. JNC 4 (1984) added a focus on systolic pressure and defined hypertension as blood pressure greater than 140/90 mm of mercury (140 systolic, 90 diastolic). JNC 7 defined "pre-hypertension" (blood pressure 120-139 systolic and/or 80-89 diastolic) and recommended stronger lifestyle approaches, such as the DASH dietary pattern. It also incorporated findings from a randomized trial that compared various classes of hypertension medications regarding their effect on cardiovascular outcomes, which was called ALLHAT (Antihypertensive and Lipid-Lowering Treatment to prevent Heart Attack Trial).

Each report was more sophisticated than the previous one, each was based on more and more scientific evidence, and each provided more detail than the last. The first JNC report had 16 pages; the seventh had 86. The first JNC report listed no references; the second listed 17; the seventh listed 386.

The National High Blood Pressure Education Program (NHBPEP) and its *Joint National Committee (JNC)* guidelines were highly successful in influencing clinical care. Based on this experience, when newly available evidence about blood cholesterol became available in the 1980s, the NHLBI created the *National Cholesterol Education Program (NCEP)*, which charged a panel of experts, called the *Adult Treatment Panel (ATP),* to develop evidence-based reports and recommendations for blood cholesterol. Separate reports released in 1988, 1993, and 2002, contained recommendations for identifying and treating high blood cholesterol, with a focus on lowering the "bad" blood cholesterol called LDL (Low-Density Lipoprotein). The NCEP reports were, as the JNC reports had been, disseminated throughout the nation, enhancing attention to cholesterol in lay and professional circles.

A single report on obesity—*the Clinical Guidelines on the Identification, Evaluation, and Treatment of Overweight and Obesity in Adults*—was released in 1998. This report established Body Mass Index (BMI) as a useful clinical measure—weight in kilograms divided by height in meters squared. It defined overweight as a BMI of 25 through 29, and obesity as a BMI of 30 or higher. The definitions were widely accepted nationally and internationally.

When I started as division director, our institute was well into the project to update these reports. The institute had invited about 70 volunteer experts from across the country to serve as members of expert panels for each of the topics. Two support contracts were approved and funded to use state-of-the-art systematic review methods to assure the updated guidelines met modern standards. The previous reports all were based on evidence, but standards for reviewing scientific evidence had changed over the years and were now more rigorous.

After I got a handle on the project status, I discussed it with my director. "We have some issues to work out," I said. "And the project is behind schedule. But a large number of people and stakeholder groups are expecting these guidelines. And the panel members already have volunteered countless hours of work."

"Can you work out the issues as you proceed?"

"I think so. We're making progress," I replied.

"Okay, then. Keep going."

And so we continued with the effort. Steps in the process included identifying key questions, determining what types of studies to look at for each question, finding all the relevant studies, assessing the quality of each study, and abstracting information from each study and entering it into a database. Once that was done, the panel members were to review the information from all the studies, decide what the findings meant for clinical practice, and write recommendations that could be implemented in clinical settings.

So, as you see, it's a long and complex process. It's not really any more complicated than the steps in developing and implementing a multi-center randomized trial (like ACCORD). But we were doing it for five topics simultaneously. It was a massive amount of work.

After months spent locating and reviewing thousands of relevant studies, it became clear that we could only address a limited number of questions. I asked the panels to reduce the number of questions to three each. That doesn't seem like many questions, but each question had multiple subparts. For example, "How low should elevated blood pressure be treated to prevent strokes?" would need to be answered in different age groups, sexes, and minority groups, making it not one but six or more questions.

We realized that the reports wouldn't need to "carry forward" recommendations from the past for which we hadn't reviewed the evidence, that they would be useful even if they were silent on some topics.

So now we were moving forward, all on the same page. But monkey wrenches were, as they say, in the works.

An investigative reporter looking at conflicts of interest in the medical field interviewed several of our panel chairs and searched for background information on panel members. He reported in *The New York Times* that the panels were full of people with conflicts of interest. Before appointing the panel members, our institute leadership had decided that more than half the members should have no conflicts, and members who had conflicts should recuse themselves from writing and voting on recommendations related to their conflicts. For example, if a member received consulting money from a pharmaceutical company, that member couldn't write or vote on recommendations about medications.

I discussed this issue thoroughly with institute leadership, and we were comfortable with our process; the approach we were using was consistent with some recommendations on how to conduct systematic literature reviews. But this conflict of interest issue, and the previous controversy about universal cholesterol screening in children, both had received damaging press. Also, as I noted previously, several guideline reports from other government-appointed bodies, like the U.S. Preventive Services Task Force, had been controversial, with the controversies widely reported in the media.

I'm not sure how much these controversies affected the decision, but my director told me that NHLBI was getting out of the guidelines business, and so our current projects would be the last clinical guidelines that our institute would sponsor.

If only I knew then what I found out later—that we should hurry up and finish the reports as quickly as possible—because more changes were in the works.

Helping People?

"We are thinking of discontinuing the community programs," a member of the institute leadership told me.

"Are you talking about the community health worker program?" I asked.

"Yes, and also the *We Can!* program."

These were programs that provided technical assistance, resources, and evidence-based information to communities across the nation to help them reduce and prevent cardiovascular disease risk factors and childhood obesity. It was 2012, and the programs had been in place for several years.

"But why?" I sked. "The funding was approved, and the contracts are in place."

"We're not sure they're a good use of our contract money."

"I'm sorry, but I don't understand. Our mission includes the application of research results, which is what these programs do. And they show that the institute is doing something to help the public."

In place before I started in my new position, these programs were a tiny fraction of the institute's budget, they helped move research findings into practice, and a lot of people relied on them. And I thought stopping the programs would be bad for the institute's reputation. So I just couldn't believe that institute leadership wanted to stop this effort.

◆ ◆ ◆

Several months before this conversation, shortly after I started as division director, I had walked into the small conference room where Karen, Matilde, Gloria, Rachel, and Jovonni were prepared to brief me on the community health worker program. The conference table was loaded with educational materials—manuals, picture cards, flip charts, recipe books, booklets, DVDs—that they had set out for me to see. It was a colorful array of educational materials with titles like *Healthy Heart, Healthy Family; With Every Heartbeat is Life;* and *Honoring the Gift of Heart Health.* I picked up a booklet and leafed through it. It contained a wealth of useful information, written in an easy-to-follow manner.

Matilde, a middle-aged Latina with olive skin, black hair, a friendly manner, and a broad grin, said we should all sit down so they could brief me on the project.

"This initiative," she said, "helps communities. They want to reduce health disparities. We help them. We train *promotores* to educate people in their communities." Promotores are community health workers who work to improve health in Hispanic communities by engaging community organizations and residents.

Karen, a woman of Italian descent with a full head of black hair peppered with some gray, and Matilde's supervisor, added, "Matilde has been the mover and shaker of this project. The materials are based on results from research. They cover blood pressure, cholesterol, diet, exercise." *Just like my lifestyle lecture,* I thought.

"We started in 1994 in the Latino community," Matilde said. "We did an early evaluation. People loved the program. So we expanded it to communities of African Americans, American Indians, Asian Americans."

"Underserved communities with health disparities," noted Karen.

Jovonni added, "I'm working on an evaluation of the program. We have data from 25 sites around the nation."

"Very impressive," I said. "I'm looking forward to learning more about this project, especially the evaluation."

At another meeting, my division staff, led by Karen, briefed me on the *We Can!* program, which stands for "Ways to Enhance Children's Activity and Nutrition. The main goal of the program was the prevention of childhood obesity, which had become a national epidemic. It was launched in 2005 based on findings from scientific literature and input from a workshop comprising about 70 experts.

Karen told me that *We Can!* not only used scientific evidence about physical activity and nutrition as they affect childhood obesity, but also used evidence from the behavioral literature on approaches to help people engage in health behaviors. The program included strategies for parents and families, organizational partners, health professionals, and media. When Michelle Obama began the *Let's Move* campaign in 2010, *We Can!* materials were shared with the White House, many of which were incorporated into, or adapted for, the *Let's Move* effort.

The materials for both of the community projects—The Community Health Worker initiative and *We Can!*—were available to the public. Limited numbers of copies were free, and communities could make however many copies they needed.

Now, at my one-on-one meeting about the programs, it seemed that a decision was still pending. So I asked, "Would it be possible to get advice from outside the institute? That's been our usual procedure for making major changes."

"Well, okay. Write up the programs using the initiative format. We'll put them on the BEE agenda." The Board of Extramural Experts was a committee of non-government experts where all proposed new initiatives were presented before they went to the Advisory Council. "The next meeting is in two weeks."

Although the timeframe was short, I was relieved to have a venue for input. I had presented to the BEE many times and not only felt comfortable doing so, I actually enjoyed it. My group and I worked feverishly to get the written descriptions in shape for the meeting.

At the BEE meeting, experts in heart, lung, and blood diseases sat around a large meeting table, microphones placed strategically around. Proposed initiatives were to be presented in the three categories of the institute's strategic plan: (1) basic science, (2) clinical science, and (3) applied science and educational programs. My division's programs fell squarely in the third category—so they would come last at the meeting. There were no other submissions for goal three for this meeting. That was not unusual since NIH's primary funding is for basic and clinical science. About 20 research initiatives were to be discussed before mine.

When it was my turn, the chair introduced me. I got up and moved to the presenter's seat where a microphone sat on the table. Before describing the community programs, I briefly explained what my division did to translate scientific results into practice. Then I described *We Can!* and the community health worker program.

A BEE member spoke up, "Your programs are terrific. There should be more of them."

Other BEE members also made positive comments. There was overwhelming support. It seemed to surprise us all. I know it surprised me.

The next day I got an email from leadership expressing concern and telling me that it didn't matter what the BEE said, that the institute's science and technology group would evaluate the programs. So, it seemed that the programs were still on the chopping block, despite the positive reaction.

The institute had been doing these kinds of translation efforts since the 1970s. They were why the institute's reputation for actually doing something for people, not just funding research, was so strong. They were why many of us had taken jobs there. Why didn't the BEE comments make a difference? Did leadership need the funding for other activities? Had presenting the programs at the BEE been a bad idea?

I was diagnosed with Parkinson's Disease the day before I got the evaluation report. It was hard to read the scathingly critical report—my hand was shaking so much.

People At The Table

A nd then we had another change in leadership, and all five division directors (of which I was one) were asked to develop talks describing our visions for the institute's future. I spent a tremendous amount of time developing my talk and getting feedback from my staff. I was asked to provide a private preview, and so I showed some of my slides to my supervisor.

"The vision is to have three national educational programs—one in heart, one in lung, one in blood," I started. "The programs would engage stakeholders in national efforts to reduce disease risk based on evidence from scientific research.

"The programs are modeled after the previous *National Cholesterol Education Program* and *National High Blood Pressure Education Program*, and the current *National Asthma Education and Prevention Program.* Those programs were tremendously successful in bringing evidence-based recommendations to every primary care doctor in the nation. The new versions would modernize the approach by expanding strategies to include policy and environments as well as education of health-care providers and people at risk.

"All of the cardiovascular risk factors—blood pressure, cholesterol, obesity, lifestyle—would be included in one comprehensive heart disease prevention program. We're calling it the National Program to Reduce Cardiovascular Risk—the NPRCR."

I was excited about the NPRCR. It was the culmination of my

career—more than the guidelines, more than the studies I had been involved in, more than anything I had done. I had been working on the concept and setting it up for a couple of years, getting it approved, funded, and in place under the previous director. I had recruited Mary, with whom I had worked on REACT and who had coordinated the National Heart Attack Alert Program, to be the program's coordinator.

"This program would coordinate looking at guidelines from various sources to come to a common agreement about messages. Then each organization would take actions consistent with their organization's mission, ranging from education to reimbursement.

"This slide lists the organizations on the NPRCR coordinating committee."

The list included government agencies like the Centers for Disease Control and Prevention (CDC), the Center for Medicaid and Medicare Services (CMS), and the Health Resources and Services Administration (HRSA). It also included national professional organizations like the American Heart Association (AHA), the American College of Cardiology (ACC), and the American Public Health Association (APHA).

My supervisor looked at the list of organizations on the slide, leaned back, looked at me, and said, "You have the wrong people at the table."

"What?" I asked, mystified.

"These are not the right organizations."

"I don't understand. These organizations have national reach. People listen to them. The list is based on decades of success in similar collaborative efforts."

"But they are not the right people."

I had no idea why they were not the "right people."

I had previously received approval to proceed. So we already had invited the organizations, and they had identified representatives—fairly high-level people within their organizations. We already had held an inaugural meeting to discuss the purpose, receive feedback, and plan next steps. A committee of the

NPRCR had nearly completed a comprehensive strategic plan that included activities at the individual, community, policy, and environmental levels. It was rather late in the process to find out we had the "wrong people."

I was sleep deprived, getting only about four hours of sleep a night for about a year due to my Parkinson's medications. I was stressed from defending the community programs and working to finish the cardiovascular guidelines. (Plus we had been told to rewrite all of our contracts, and I had vacancies that I couldn't fill. And my mother was dying.)

I tried to hold back, but I couldn't. I started to cry.

"I need to tell you something," I said, wiping my eyes. "I have Parkinson's Disease, and I'm thinking of stepping down as division director. This position is just too stressful. Stress makes my symptoms worse. It isn't good for my health."

"I understand. Thanks for telling me. I'll look into finding you another position suited to your talents."

As I walked home that evening, my left arm felt stiff. My left hand shook. My left leg felt awkward and uncoordinated. I felt unbalanced, afraid of falling again. And tears streamed down my face.

So much time and effort, so many contributions from lots of talented people. So many good ideas. Everything seemed to be falling apart. I was devastated.

I remained the division director for a while, but I was excluded from decision-making about the cardiovascular guidelines. I heard that arrangements were being made for the American Heart Association to take over the project. I didn't know whether that was because the NIH director said NIH shouldn't be in the guidelines business (which I heard second hand) or whether it was because the draft reports contained controversial recommendations. Or maybe it was both. Or something else.

The new draft recommendations for treating blood choles-terol did not focus on LDL cholesterol (the "bad" cholesterol) as in the past. Instead, the recommendation was to give statin medication (which reduces risk) to people at high risk regardless of their LDL level. The expert panel made this change because none of the randomized trials had tested lowering cholesterol to a target LDL level. Instead, the trials had com-pared a statin to a placebo or compared different statins or different doses in people judged to be at high risk. So, this new recommendation was more consistent with evidence from ran-domized trials.

The panel had updated a risk assessment equation to define high risk. The equation included age, sex, race, cholesterol level, blood pressure level, diabetes, and smoking. The draft guidelines recommended that adults with greater than 7.5% risk of having a cardiovascular event (heart attack, stroke, or cardiovascular death) over ten years be put on a statin. The 7.5% figure was obtained from the actual risk of patients in control groups of the randomized trials. This was an entirely new—and controversial—way to treat blood cholesterol.

For blood pressure, the long-standing goal of systolic pres-sure less than 140 was jettisoned in persons over age 60 because the expert panel did not think randomized trials supported that goal. Instead, they recommended treating systolic pres-sure to less than 150 in that age group. They also abandoned a previous lower blood pressure goal in people with diabetes for lack of trial evidence.

These may seem like small changes to someone not in the field, but they were viewed by some experts as dramatic and they were highly controversial.

Regardless of the controversies I thought we should publish the guidelines for several reasons: we were using high-quality methods, we had made a commitment to the expert volunteers working on the project, our stakeholders (other organizations and the medical community) were awaiting the results, and completing the project would sustain the institute's excellent reputation in translating scientific findings into practice.

But now, despite five years of work, donated time and expertise from 70 experts, funding of several million dollars of taxpayer money, and institute staff working feverishly for years, I heard that our institute was not going to publish the reports and was giving the project away. The institute's executive committee never discussed the issue, although it had been on the agenda.

My supervisor officially removed me from the guidelines project. I abandoned the vision of three national education programs because of lack of support.

And my Parkinson's symptoms kept getting worse.

My Dilemma

I had so very much wanted to do this job, working on translating scientific findings into practice—a job that was the culmination of my career. Despite my Parkinson's and the stress at work, I had kept plugging away, trying to get things done—for three years after my diagnosis.

I had learned many years prior, when I decided to go back to medical school, not to give up. Now it seemed I had no choice. I wasn't being kicked out—in fact, I received an excellent performance rating. But nearly every project in our division was threatened to be axed.

Not only that, but I was the only division director not invited to be a member of a new committee that would plan institute directions. My supervisor asked me not to attend a retreat to discuss future efforts in implementation and translation research—an area I had pursued for decades and for which I had provided suggestions for moving forward. I never did get that new position I thought I would get. And, a real sting, the institute was creating a new center for implementation and translation research—without me.

I was shut out. Why? Because I had said I was going to step down as a division director? Because I was the only woman division director? Because I had Parkinson's? Because I argued with leadership? Because I didn't stop the community programs? All of these things? Something else?

I imagine that, behind the scenes, I was perceived as a

problem employee. But I was just trying to do my job—a job at a level in the organizational structure that I had (erroneously) assumed would give me some authority. But now, a job that was gradually being taken away.

There's a joke that goes something like this: A man goes away on vacation and asks his neighbor to watch his house and check on his cat and his mother, who lives with him. Calling in from vacation, the man asks, 'How's my cat?' The neighbor tells him that the cat got out of the house and climbed up onto the roof. Then he fell off the roof and hobbled across the street, where he was hit by a car and died. The man on vacation says, 'I wish you had told me a little at a time, so I could get used to the news. First, you could have told me my cat was on the roof. Then the next time I called that the cat fell off and was hurt. Then later, the cat had died.' 'Oh, I understand,' says the neighbor. 'So how's my mother?' asks the man on vacation. 'Well,' the neighbor says, 'Your mother's on the roof.'

So I said to Bruce that evening, "Today I told my division that I have Parkinson's Disease. That their mother's on the roof. I don't think I can stay there any longer."

And so, in 2013, the American Heart Association published the cholesterol and obesity guidelines and the risk assessment report. The high blood pressure panel published their report independently. Our institute did publish evidence reviews but took no stand on recommendations.

I suspect that NIH leadership shied away from publishing the reports because of controversial recommendations in them. But there are always controversies about what evidence means for practice. Though new studies come out all the time, more research is always needed to fill in evidence gaps.

When we can't see the whole picture, can't we use what we do see to inform practice? I think that we can—that we must. Otherwise, why are we doing the research?

I did want to finish and publish the guidelines. But more important to me—and to our institute, I thought—were the national educational programs for heart, lung, and blood conditions. We could provide real leadership by creating venues where different organizations, governmental and non-governmental, could hash out differences in opinions, develop common messages, and take complementary actions toward the same goals. But as far as I know, the new programs never had another meeting.

The stress of my disease, side effects of medications, lack of sleep, complicated bureaucracy, and lack of support for my division's projects made it impossible to accomplish what I had hoped. So it should have been easy to let go.

But at the same time, it was difficult to let go, as this job was the culmination of my life's work—four decades of applied clinical research to inform practice. So we can help people.

For several days I had been experiencing chest discomfort. So when Bruce walked in from work one evening, I asked him to take me to the Emergency Room. My ECG had some minor abnormalities, so they kept me overnight for monitoring.

The test for myocardial enzymes, which rise when you have a heart attack, came back normal. So I hadn't had a heart attack. The hospital sent me home the next morning with instructions to follow up with a cardiologist and to get a stress test, which turned out normal.

I told Bruce that, having been in charge of the REACT trial (which, as you remember, was to educate people to seek care soon when they had heart attack symptoms), I would have been embarrassed if I had died because I ignored the chest discomfort!

The chest pain and visit to the ER made it clear to me that I needed to make some changes. There was no new position for me in the works at NHLBI—I would have liked to work on implementation research there—so I decided to take a job elsewhere at NIH, a job with less responsibility, a stepping-stone to retirement.

I was supposed to announce my leaving at a combined meeting of our division and two other groups, who would now be working together more closely under (another) reorganization.

Before that larger meeting, I called my division staff of about 15 into my office for a smaller meeting. I closed the door, looked around at them, and told them that I was leaving the institute. I wanted them to know first.

My left hand shook. My left arm was stiff. I cried. Some of us hugged.

Then we all went to the combined larger meeting, where I announced that I was moving to another spot in NIH, pretended everything was fine, and publically shook the hand of the person who appeared to be my replacement.

Several weeks later, NHLBI held a goodbye party for me. People from our institute attended as well as people from other institutes with whom I had worked. My husband and son came also.

Mary gave a hilarious roast. Then they passed the microphone around so people could say something if they wanted to. I teared up as many people said nice things about me. I was particularly pleased that many of them acknowledged what I had been trying to do for 20-odd years—develop evidence to inform practice. And several people noted that I had hired them. I had forgotten how many there had been.

Then I gave a humorous PowerPoint presentation about how long I had been there—highlighting changes that had occurred in the world over 20 years—and culminating in the trailer for *NHLBI: The Movie.*

Over about three years, I had experienced a massive amount of stress. I was diagnosed with Parkinson's; I had sciatica and was barely able to walk for several months; we moved from our four-bedroom house to a two-bedroom condo; I oversaw the care of my 98-year-old dying mother; and I took a stressful new position where all my projects were disapproved, given away, or threatened to be discontinued.

I took an online assessment of perceived stress and scored in the highest category. I tried working at another office at NIH for several months. But a two-week government shutdown made me realize that I had to retire.

My heart wasn't in it any more. Now I had to take care of myself.

EPILOGUE: WHO AM I NOW?

S o who am I now, without my work that defined me for decades?

I am a "housewife" who sweeps the kitchen floor in the morning when the sun streams in through the east-facing windows so I can see the crumbs and dust on the floor. I find that routine tasks requiring no thought, like sweeping, can be comforting.

I am a cook, who has supper ingredients prepped—or if it's soup or chili, the dish cooking slowly in a crockpot—by the time Bruce gets home from work.

As part of a self-prescribed rehabilitation program, I build Lego buildings, crochet, and do crossword puzzles—some with my left (Parkinson's) hand.

I watch a fair amount of television, sometimes in the afternoons by myself, or in the evenings with Bruce. I watched every West Wing episode in order from the beginning—one afternoon I spent an hour sitting on the couch in front of the TV with tears rolling down my cheeks when Josh had PTSD after being shot in an assassination attempt on President Bartlett. I thought I understood how he felt.

I sometimes go to a movie by myself at the spur of the moment to an afternoon matinee. This year I saw all the best-picture nominees except for one. A movie theater is within walking distance, as are a slew of restaurants, a bookstore, a couple of grocery stores, clothing stores, shoe stores, and other shops. I do a lot of walking.

I've been reading a lot also—from memoirs to science fiction, from classics to current best sellers. And science books, like Darwin's "The Origin of the Species by Means of Natural Selection," and Brian Greene's "The Fabric of the Cosmos."

For a while, I was Zumina, my avatar in the role-playing game called Kingdom Age®. I played it on my iPhone every day, including the first thing in the morning and the last thing at night. As Zumina, I was a killer of beasts and a warrior. In Kingdom Age®, I was part of a team, called a guild, comprising 60 players across the world. In the game, I was healthy.

After being retired for a few years, most of my Parkinson's symptoms are pretty much stable and controlled by medication and exercise.

I'm on a new form of Sinemet, called Rytary, which includes both short- and delayed-action levodopa and carbidopa. I need to take Rytary every four hours while awake. I set alarms on my phone to remind me. I can feel when the medication wears off—tremor, stiffness, uncoordination, poor balance, and aching muscles return.

I've gone back to exercising vigorously. I exercise every morning: Jazzercise (aerobic dance) two days a week, a resistance training (weights) two days a week , and walking, indoor cycling, and yoga on other days. I think of exercising as my job. It makes a huge difference for the Parkinson's symptoms. The single-subject non-randomized study of exercise, of which I'm the only participant, is a success so far. So physically I'm doing quite well.

When I'm medicated and have exercised that day, I almost feel normal. That is, unless I feel stressed. More things stress me than previously, and anxiety seems to negate the effects of the medication. I'm not so good anymore around crowds, and I prefer to sit at home. I have to make myself go to social events.

I try to keep my stress level low. I've found online Parkinson's support groups. We share with each other and help each other get through this disease.

And now I have new joy in my life—a darling granddaughter.

Thinking back on my career, I'm proud of what I was able to accomplish, while at the same time disappointed. I had hoped to make a contribution, but I'm not sure how much I actually contributed.

The studies I was involved in did provide some evidence about strategies to prevent cardiovascular diseases, but most of the studies had unimportant findings in and of themselves. However, evidence provided by one study does not a conclusion make. It's critical to look at a whole body of evidence—as we did when conducting systematic reviews of the scientific literature. Although some of the conclusions were controversial, identifying controversies is one way for science to advance, as it points to areas needing further study.

NIH primarily focuses on basic science research—studies done in laboratories with cells, genes, proteins, microbes, and/or animals. A contingent of NIH staff, however, is interested in research with human subjects that can directly inform public health or clinical practice the day the results are released. I am proud of having stimulated and worked on many studies in this arena of applied research for public health and clinical practice.

I was ambitious to attain a position where I could make a more significant contribution, but when I finally did, symptomatic Parkinson's and difficult bureaucracy hobbled my efforts.

I wonder how many other people are in similar situations—how much talent goes untapped because of health issues or clashes with bureaucracy.

After I retired, I did a few small consulting jobs—a couple of talks at NIH and on a peer-review committee for grant applications. And I worked for a few months, part-time at eight hours a week, on a prevention research project for NIH at a different institute. But I found that work to be too stressful and so I resigned.

Should I be doing something completely different now that I have the chance—like taking art lessons?

Or maybe I'll write a memoir and share some of what I learned.

Acknowledgments

T hough I felt compelled to write about my life, I also found it challenging to do so. I appreciate all the advice, feedback, and support I received from many people.

First, I would like to thank my husband, Bruce Simons-Morton, for supporting me throughout my career and my life-changing diagnosis of Parkinson's disease. Bruce and I have been equal partners, together for almost 40 years. I cannot thank him enough for reading numerous drafts, putting up with me talking about my memoir nearly daily (for years!), helping me figure out how to present some content, helping me deal with my Parkinson's, and being an all-around good sport about it all. Bruce, I couldn't have done any of it without you!

Several friends and family members read complete drafts and gave me excellent feedback. My sister, Diane Thornton, a published author herself, was an immense help in providing detailed feedback (including crossing out entire paragraphs as "boring" and helping me decide on self-publishing). My sister, Doreen Peri, did a terrific job proofreading the manuscript and helping me write the blurb on the back of the paperback version. My other sister, Donna Simons, also helped with the book cover. Colleagues and friends who read the whole draft and gave me terrific feedback include Jeff Cutler ("I'm glad you're writing this"), Tamara Bavendam ("you had it all"), Ron Knipling ("what about heritability?"), and Tom Gardosik ("it's a good story").

My son, Don Morton, helped me work on the style of writing

by parsing specific sections and reminding me to "show not tell." My daughter, Bahia Simons-Lane, gave me general feedback and provided emotional support. Bruce, Diane, Doreen, and Don worked on the title with me, brainstorming and vetting about a dozen different draft titles.

In addition to those mentioned above, I would like to acknowledge my teachers, supervisors, and colleagues who helped me in my career, including Roger Sherwin, Irving Kessler, Guy Parcel, Pat Mullen, Fred Annegers, Carlos Vallbona, Karen Donato, and Peter Savage.

And lots of thanks to neurologists Dr. Satinsky and Dr. Ellenstein who diagnosed and treated my Parkinson's, Dr. Andrew, my primary care physician, who jumped on my symptoms and ordered tests, and Elizabeth E. Rankin, my therapist, who made me realize that having a deadline could actually reduce my stress.

I also thank the Writers' Center in Bethesda, Maryland, where I took courses on creative nonfiction and the publishing process.

And I'd like to acknowledge all the patients and their caregivers that suffer from the ravages of Parkinson's disease. You are not alone.

APPENDIX: FOR MORE INFORMATION

<u>Principles And Models</u>

Green LW; Kreuter MW; Deeds SG; Partridge KB; Bartlett E. *Health Education Planning: A Diagnostic Approach.* (PRECEDE) Palo Alto, California, Mayfield Publishing, 1980

Simons-Morton DG, Simons-Morton BG, Parcel GS, Bunker JF. Influencing Personal and Environmental Conditions for Community Health: A Multilevel Intervention Model. (MATCH) *Family and Community Health.* 11(2):25-35, 1988

Hill AB. The Environment and Disease: Association or Causation? *Proceedings of the Royal Society of Medicine.* 58(5): 295–300, 1965

Friedman L, Simons-Morton DG, Cutler JA. Comparative Features of Primordial, Primary, and Secondary Prevention Trials. In Manson J, Buring JE, Ridker PM, Gaziano JM (eds.) *Clinical Trials in Heart Disease: A Companion to Braunwald's Heart Disease*, 2nd edition, 2004

<u>Research Studies</u>

The ACCORD Study Group (writing group: Gerstein HC, Miller ME, Byington RP, Goff DC, Bigger T, Buse JB, Cushman WC, Genuth S, Ismail-Beigi F, Grimm RH, Probstfield JL, Simons-Morton DG, Friedewald WT). Effects of Intensive Glucose Lowering in Type 2 Diabetes. *New Eng J Medicine* 358:2545-59, 2008

The ACCORD Study Group (Ginsberg HN, Elam MB, Lovato LC, Crouse JR, Leiter LA, Linz P, Friedewald WT, Buse JB, Gerstein HC, Probstfield J, Grimm RH, Ismail-Beigi F, Bigger JT, Goff DC, Cushman WC, Simons-Morton DG, Byington RP). Effects of combination lipid therapy in type 2 diabetes mellitus. *New Eng J Medicine*, 362:1563-74, 2010

The ACCORD Study Group (Cushman WC, Evans GW, Byington RP, Goff DC, Grimm RH, Cutler JA, Simons-Morton DG, Basile JN, Corson MA, Probstfield JL, Katz L, Peterson KA, Friedewald WT, Buse JB, Bigger JT, Gerstein HC, Ismail-Beigi F). Effects of intensive blood-pressure control in type 2 diabetes mellitus. *New Eng J Medicine*, 362:1575-85, 2010

The Writing Group for the Activity Counseling Trial Research Group [Simons-Morton DG, Blair SN, King AC, Morgan TM, Applegate WG, O'Toole M, Haskell WL, Albright CL, Cohen SJ, Ribisl PM, Shih JH]. Effects of physical activity counseling in primary care: The Activity Counseling Trial: A randomized controlled trial. *J Amer Med Assoc (JAMA)* 286:677-687 2001

Diabetes Prevention Program Research Group. Reduction in the incidence of type 2 diabetes with lifestyle intervention or metformin. *New Eng J Medicine* 346:393-403, 2002

Appel L, Moore T, Obarzanek E, Vollmer W, Svetkey L, Sacks F, Bray G, Vogt T, Cutler JA, Windhauser M, Lin P, Karanja N, Simons-Morton DG, et al. A clinical trial of the effects of dietary patterns on blood pressure. [DASH] *New Eng J Medicine* 336:1117-1124, 1997

Sacks FM, Svetkey LP, Vollmer WM, Appel LJ, Bray GA, Harsha D, Obarzanek E, Conlin PR, Miller ER, Simons-Morton DG, Karanja N, Lin P-H, for the DASH-Sodium Collaborative Research Group. Effects on blood pressure of reduced dietary sodium and the dietary approaches to stop hypertension (DASH) Diet. *New Eng J Medicine* 344:3-10, 2001

Five-year findings of the Hypertension Detection and Follow-up Program [HDFP]: Reduction in mortality of persons with high blood pressure, including mild hypertension. *J Amer Med Assoc (JAMA)* 277(2):157-166, 1979

Lipid Research Clinics Program. Primary Prevention Trial results: Reduction in incidence of coronary heart disease. *J Amer Med Assoc (JAMA)* 25:351-364, 1984

Mullen PD, Simons-Morton DG, Ramirez G, Frankowski RF, Green LW, Mains DA. A meta-analysis of trials evaluating patient education and counseling for three groups of preventive behaviors. *Patient Education and Counseling* 32(3):157-173, 1997

Simons-Morton DG, Donato K, Loria CM, Pratt CA, Ershow AG, Morrissette MA, Czajkowski S, Arteaga SS, Obarzanek E. Obesity research and programs at the National Heart, Lung, and Blood Institute. *J Am Coll Cardiol* 55(9):917-920, 2010

Luepker RV, Raczynski JM, Osganian S, Goldberg RJ, Finnegan JR, Hedges JR, Goff DC, Eisenberg MS, Zapka JG, Feldman HA, Labarthe DR, McGovern PG, Cornell CE, Proschan MA, Simons-Morton DG. Effect of a community intervention on patient delay and emergency medical service use in acute coronary heart disease: The Rapid Early Action for Coronary Treatment (REACT) trial. *J Amer Med Assoc (JAMA)* 284:60-67, 2000

Educational Programs, Recommendations, Guidelines

Kavey RE, Simons-Morton DG, de Jesus JM: Supplement Editors. Daniels SR, Benuck I, Christakis DA, Dennison BA, Gidding SS, Gillman MW, Gottesman MM, Kwiterovich PO, McBride PE, McCrindle BW, Roccini AP, Urbina EM, Van Horn LV, Washington RL. Expert panel on integrated guidelines for cardiovascular health and risk reduction for children and adolescents: Summary Report. *Pediatrics*, 128:Suppl 5;S213-S256, 2011

Eckel RH, Jakicic JM, Ard JD, Hubbard VS, de Jesus JM, Lee I-M, Lichtenstein AH, et al. 2013 AHA/ACC guidelines on lifestyle management to reduce cardiovascular risk: A report of the American College of Cardiology/American Heart Association Task Force on Practice Guidelines. *Circulation* 129(25 Suppl 2):S76-99, 2014

2013 ACC/AHA Guidelines on the treatment of blood cholesterol to reduce atherosclerotic cardiovascular risk in adults: A report of the American College of Cardiology/American Heart Association Task Force on Practice Guidelines. *Circulation* 129(25 Suppl 2):S1-45, 2013

U.S. Department of Agriculture and U.S. Department of Health and Human Services. *Dietary Guidelines for Americans, 2010*. 7th Edition, Washington, DC: U.S. Government Printing Office, December 2010

Tricoci P, Allen JM, Kramer JM, Califf RM, Smith SC. Scientific evidence underlying the ACC/AHA clinical practice guidelines. *J Amer Med Assoc (JAMA)*. 2009;301(8):831-841

James PA, Oparil S, Carter BL, Cushman WC, Dennison-Himmelfarb C, Handler J, Lackland DT, LeFevre ML, MacKenzie TC, Ogedegbe O, Smith SC, Svetkey LP, Taler S, Townsend RR, Wright JT, Narva AS, Ortiz E. 2014 Evidence-based guideline for the management of high blood pressure in adults: Report from the panel members appointed to the Eighth Joint National Committee (JNC 8) *J Amer Med Assoc (JAMA)* 311(5):507-520, 2014

Hand M, Brown C, Horan M, Simons-Morton D. The National Heart Attack Alert Program: Progress at five years in educating providers, patients, and the public and future directions. *J Thromb Thrombolysis* 6(1):9-17, 1998

Expert Panel on Detection, Evaluation, and Treatment of High Blood Cholesterol in Adults. Executive summary of The Third Report of The National Cholesterol Education Program. *J Amer Med Assoc (JAMA)* 2001 May 16;285(19):2486-97, 2001

(NCEP) Expert Panel on Detection, Evaluation, and Treatment of High Blood Cholesterol in Adults (Adult Treatment Panel III). *J Amer Med Assoc (JAMA)* 285(19):2486-9, 2001

Jones DW. The National High Blood Pressure Education Program: Thirty years and counting. *Hypertension* 39:941-942, 2002

Jensen MD, Ryan DH, Apovian CM, Ard JD, Comuzzzie, Donato KA, et al. 2013 AHA/ACC/TOS guideline for the management of overweight and obesity in adults: A report of the American College of Cardiology/American Heart Association Task Force on Practice Guidelines and the Obesity Society. *Circulation* 129(25 Suppl 2):S102-38, 2014

Behavioral Weight Loss Interventions to Prevent Obesity-Related Morbidity and Mortality in Adults US Preventive Services Task Force Recommendation Statement. Journal of the American Medical Association (JAMA). 2018;320(11):1163-1171, 2018

Physical Activity Guidelines Writing Group (Buchner DM, Bishop J, Brown DR, Fulton JE, Galuska DA, Gilchrist J, Guralnik JM, Hootman JM, Johnson MA, Kohl HW, Lee SM, Loughrey KA, McDivitt JA, Simons-Morton DG, Smith AW, Tilson WM, Troiano RP, Wargo JD, Willis GB). *2008 Physical Activity Guidelines for Americans.* ODPHP Publication No. U0036, October 2008

U.S. Preventive Services Task Force. Screening for breast cancer: U.S. Preventive Services Task Force recommendation statement. *Archives of Internal Medicine.* 151;716-26, 2009

U.S. Preventive Services Task Force. Counseling and interventions to prevent tobacco use and tobacco-caused disease in adults and pregnant women: U.S. Preventive Services Task Force Reaffirmation Recommendation Statement. *Archives of Internal Medicine.* 150:551-555, 2009

Moyer VA on behalf of the U.S. Preventive Services Task Force. Screening for Prostate Cancer: U.S. Preventive Services Task Force Recommendation Statement. *Annals of Internal Medicine.* 157(2):120-134, 2012

Improving Delivery of Preventive Interventions in Clinical Practice: Practical Implications and Future Research Directions. NHLBI Workshop Report, 2009. https://www.nhlbi.nih.gov/events/2009/improving-cardiovascular-disease-prevention

Made in the USA
Middletown, DE
11 May 2023

30357217R00175